Kairos

From Exclusivity to Commonalities

With Moral Respect

By Albert Gentleman

Copyright © Albert Gentleman 2025

All rights reserved. Other than for the purposes and subject to the conditions prescribed under the Copyright Act, no part of this publication may be reproduced, stored in a retrieval system, or transmitted in any form or by any means, electronic, mechanical, photocopying, recording or otherwise, without the prior permission of the publisher.

This book is a work of non-fiction.

ISBN: 9781763737433

Table of Contents

Prologue   5

Part 1 – Kairos: A Common Universal Way   9

1 Before Kairos – The Commonalities   11

2 What is Kairos?   21

3 Principles and Values of Kairos   27

4 The Inner Shift   37

5 Navigating Harmful Beliefs and Practices   45

6 Which One is the One True Religion?   51

Part 2: The Journey That Led Me Here   59

7 The Turning Point: A Morning in Yangon   61

8 A Religious Childhood and My Exploring Nature   67

9 Leaving Home, Seeking Life   71

10 Turning Toward Faith   77

11 The Missionary Years Begin   81

12 Twelve Years in Seven Countries   87

13 The Breaking Point in Myanmar   95

14 Freedom in Laos   97

15 Returning Home, Living The Kairos Way   101

Final Words   105

Appendix Introduction   109

Appendix 1	My Questions and Discoveries	111
Appendix 2	My Evolving Beliefs	129
Appendix 3	Rethinking Divine Justice	137
Appendix 4	Final Reflections – Values That Endure	139

Prologue

__Kairos (n.):__ Kairos is an ancient Greek term that refers to a moment of insightful opportunity or transformation - the right, awakening moment when life opens, and there is change

This book is both an alternative and a story.

It offers an alternative to cultural and spiritual exclusivity, a vision where our cultures and belief systems can honour moral differences and still come together in friendship, based on what we share. I call these shared values *Commonalities*, the principles and values that unite us across traditions and worldviews. Together, we'll reflect on the deeper questions of life, faith, and our shared humanity, wherever you are in your personal journey.

And it's a story, my own story, of how, after thirty-six years as a devoted Christian, I left Christianity. Those years included twelve as a missionary in seven Southeast Asian countries, and gradually the beliefs I once held as absolute no longer fit the truths I was discovering.

I didn't walk away in anger, but in honesty.

What followed was a slow and sacred shift, what I later came to call a **Kairos moment**.

You may have heard of the Greek word **Kairos**, an ancient word meaning the "right" or "opportune" moment, a time when life opens and something within begins to awaken.

For me, Kairos isn't just a new opportunity; it's an invitation, to step beyond boundaries, to see what we share, and to walk toward one another instead of apart.

This book is divided into two parts:

- **Part One – Kairos: A Common Universal Way** lays out the values, principles, and perspectives I've come to see as shared across many cultural and spiritual traditions, what I believe can serve as a unifying path forward for people from all backgrounds.

- **Part Two – The Journey That Led Me Here** shares the personal story behind that vision: my years in faith, the questions that stirred, the discoveries that shifted everything, and the freedom that followed.

Through these pages, I invite you to walk with me, not toward a new religion, but toward a renewed way of seeing. We'll explore the common threads running through different cultures and beliefs: love, wisdom, compassion, truth, and the recognition of a universal presence I call the **Precious Spirit**.

This book is written in a conversational style, like a quiet moment in a park or a warm chat in a café. I hope it feels that way to you: informal, thoughtful, and open. You're welcome to agree, to question, to reflect, and to discover at your own pace.

Above all, this book is about moral respect:

- Respect for the diverse tapestry of moral human beliefs.
- Respect for the common ground we all share.
- And respect for the sacred thread that runs through all of life.

- And moral respect, a conscious regard for human dignity and the well-being of our planet, while refusing to approve beliefs or actions that cause harm. These we cannot respect.

So, take your time. Let the words settle. This isn't a destination. It's a journey, and I'm honored to walk it with you.

Part 1

Kairos: A Common Universal Way

Chapter 1

Before Kairos: The Commonalities

Before I gave it a name, before I stepped away from the structures I had once embraced, I began to sense something universal beneath the surface of all spiritual paths, something older than doctrine and wider than belief.

Across many years and cultures, I found myself walking beside people of vastly different faiths such as Muslims, Buddhists, Hindus, Indigenous elders, Free Thinkers, even those who claimed no faith at all. And yet, time and again, I noticed something quietly astonishing: so many of us shared the same heart values such as love, honesty, kindness, generosity, respect for life and the longing for connection and community.

Even when our beliefs differed, our inner compass often pointed in the same direction.

There was no single label for this shared space, no denomination or dogma could fully contain it, yet I began to feel it was *sacred*. Not in the sense of rituals or temples, but in the way people lived out compassion in daily life. In the way a Muslim café owner fed a stranger. In the compassion of a Buddhist monk caring for poor people infected with HIV. In the laughter of children from every tradition. In the still, quiet moments when Spirit seemed to speak through silence itself.

Looking back, I now see that these encounters were preparing me. They were softening the ground for a deeper awakening. They were reminding me that there is something beautiful and binding at the root of all cultures, something that existed long before I stepped into the framework of Christianity, and something that remained long after I stepped out.

And it is here, in these shared commonalities, that the journey toward Kairos truly begins.

Before I introduce Kairos more fully, I want to share how the idea first began to take shape in my heart and mind. It didn't come all at once. It was more like a slow unfolding, a gentle pulling back of the veil. A quiet invitation to step outside the lines I had drawn around my Christian beliefs, and into something more expansive, more life-giving, and more real. I was being exposed to so many wonderful people of different cultures and beliefs and they were mostly very kind and friendly. I sensed that we had something in common, something that grounded us, namely our principles and values for life.

These shared moral principles and values, what I call **Commonalities**, became clearer during my latter years in Southeast Asia. As I worked in remote villages and bustling cities, I was welcomed into homes, temples, mosques, and community gatherings. I built friendships grounded in kindness, mutual respect, moral integrity and love, the very same principles I found in most cultures.

I also began to notice another commonality. In the gaze of a Hindu priest in Mumbai, the chants of a Buddhist monk at Shwedagon Pagoda in Yangon, and the prayers of a Muslim imam in Brunei, I sensed a shared longing, a universal desire to connect with something greater, beyond ourselves. It made me wonder: despite all our cultural and religious differences, could we all be reaching toward the same eternal source, the same universal Presence, what I now call the *Precious Spirit*. It moves through all sincere expressions of love and truth, no matter the name or language used.

It wasn't the differences that stood out to me, but the similarities, the quiet harmony that seemed to underlie all these cultures.

These insights gently expanded my understanding of culture and spirituality. They softened or removed the boundaries I had once believed were fixed. As someone who had spent years in missionary work, once convinced that only Christianity held the truth, this shift was no small matter.

Over time, I came to see spiritual truths as a vast river, fed by many streams, each offering its own beauty, wisdom, and insight. While the details may differ, such as beliefs, names for the divine, and rituals, the core human longing for peace, provision, meaning, community, love, and respect runs through them all. That realization brought me a sense of connection and clarity. It helped me appreciate the richness of humanity's spiritual and cultural diversity, not as something to fear or reject, but as something I can learn from.

As I began to notice these similarities across faiths and cultures, I started to reflect more deeply on the values that seemed to show up again and again, no matter where I was or who I was speaking with. These shared values pointed to something deeper, an ethical core that many spiritual paths held in common. It was as if, underneath all the differences, there was a shared moral compass, a kind of quiet agreement about what it means to live a good life. That's when I began to think of these as more than coincidences. They were common truths, universal principles, a way of being.

Morality Without Borders

As I look back on those years, one thing becomes clear: understanding, truth and goodness are not limited to any one religion. For centuries, spiritual teachers from many cultures have pointed to the same basic values, values that cross all boundaries of language, culture, and belief.

These include:

- Love and compassion
- Goodness and kindness
- Giving and generosity
- Humility and self-control
- Fairness, mercy, and justice for all
- Respect for life
- Care for the poor and vulnerable

These are not just religious teachings. They are human values and principles that have helped people get through hard times, solve conflicts, and build better lives together. Though spiritual paths use different words and stories, the heart of their teachings is often the same.

The more I encountered these shared values, the more my love and respect grew for people of other faiths. My view of the world expanded, and I found real joy in learning from others.

In time, I came to believe that underneath all our religious differences, many spiritual paths are drawing from the same deep well of compassion, wisdom, and ethical integrity. This new way of seeing, what I later came to call **Kairos**, is not about saying all religions are the same. They're not. Each tradition has its own sacred stories, its own symbols and practices. But something deeper connects them.

I began to realise, when we stop trying to prove who is right, we start to see what we share. And instead of asking, *"Which path is correct?"*, I found myself asking new questions: *"What can I learn if I stop defending and start listening?" "What truth might I find in another person's journey?"*

Letting go of rivalry didn't mean giving up my own beliefs. It meant holding them more gently, with humility, understanding that they are one part of a much bigger picture. And that picture, when seen in its fullness, was more beautiful than anything I had known before.

Letting Go of the Old God

As I stepped further away from the rigid framework of my former faith, I began to look at the figure of Jesus with fresh eyes, not as a divine being descended from heaven to fulfill ancient prophecy, but as a deeply awakened human being whose life radiated compassion, courage, and spiritual clarity. I saw him not as someone sent to uphold the harsh commands of an ancient deity, but as someone who, in his own time, reimagined the Divine in ways that were tender, just, and radically inclusive. His teachings often stood in contrast to the more violent or judgmental images of God found in earlier texts. Rather than quoting scripture to dominate, he used it to liberate. Rather than reinforcing religion, he invited people into a deeper, more personal connection with what many now call the Source, that timeless, universal Presence that exists beyond names, beyond doctrine, and beyond borders. Whether one believes in Jesus, follows another tradition, or walks a path free of religion altogether, I believe the Spirit he embodied points us toward the same sacred reality: a Presence not of fear or control, but of love, awareness, and inner freedom. And with this new vision of Spirit came a quiet invitation, not to believe harder, but to live more consciously, more lovingly, more awake.

Conscious Living

If the Sacred is not confined to one religion, and if no single tradition owns the truth, then how we live, our choices, our awareness, our relationships, becomes the sacred ground where spirituality takes root. I began to see that many traditions hold a similar belief: that something deeper lives within us, not that we are always good or unbroken, but that beneath the surface, there is a spark, a capacity, a potential to respond to love, truth, and conscience. This inner presence, what some call Spirit, doesn't mean people always live in harmony with it. We all fall short. But it suggests that beneath even our most harmful choices, there remains a quiet invitation, to return, to grow, to be transformed. To live consciously is to stay open to that possibility, both in ourselves and in others. Some call it mindfulness. Others speak of walking in the Spirit, flowing with the Tao, or honouring ancestors through daily actions.

Whatever the name, the desire is the same:

- To live purely and with care.
- To pay attention to intuition.
- To be honest and open with yourself.
- To let truth, and for many, the sacred guide your steps.
- To intercede on behalf of others

For me, this conscious living in the form of meditation means being aware of how my actions affect both myself and others, how my beliefs shape the world, and how my inner life connects with something greater. I'm far from perfect, sometimes I slip into selfishness or forget my deeper values, but when I take a moment and pause in life or even meditate, I live with more awareness and integrity. Life feels more grounded, more joyful, and more whole.

Part of conscious living is being open to what is true, seeing things as they really are, not just how we were taught to see them or wish them to be. Sometimes truth comes gently through quiet reflection in moments of stillness, meditation, or solitude, when we're finally able to hear the deeper voice within us. These moments can bring clarity, showing us something we hadn't fully noticed before.

Other times, truth arrives like a jolt, a sudden wake-up call that disrupts our usual way of thinking. It might come through a difficult experience, a surprising conversation, or something we witness that shakes us deeply. These moments can feel uncomfortable or even painful, but they often lead to powerful growth.

And sometimes, truth comes through research, listening to critical thinking scholars and asking questions. This kind of truth-seeking can be eye-opening. We must be willing to challenge what we've been taught and to follow the new evidence, even if it leads us in unexpected directions.

That's what happened to me. While living in Myanmar, I began to explore the doubts I had about some of the Christian beliefs I once held as absolute. What I discovered surprised me. Some beliefs weren't true at all; others were only partly true. The more I questioned, the more I began to see with clearer eyes.

Letting go of those beliefs wasn't easy. It felt like losing part of who I was. But in releasing them, something new took root. My heart softened. My compassion deepened. Life became more connected and honest. It wasn't about rejecting everything I'd believed, it was about being open and letting truth and awareness guide me toward a fuller, freer way of living.

This kind of openness doesn't mean agreeing with everything. What is true still has boundaries. It means having the courage to face difficult truths with wisdom, and the openness and understanding to let new wisdom guide us in a better direction. This is part of conscious living. For some, this might still include parts of their religious tradition. For others, it may lead them away from religion altogether. What matters most isn't the label we wear, but the presence, honesty, and love with which we live.

These shared principles and values; kindness, justice, generosity, integrity, reverence, and conscious living, became part of the foundation of what I would later call *Kairos*. They weren't new ideas, but enduring truths from many traditions.

A New Kind of Unity

In today's world, where so much division comes from religion, power, and selfishness, I believe what we need is not sameness, but a new kind of unity, one built on our shared values and *moral respect.*

By *moral respect*, I mean holding deep regard for people's dignity, safety, and the well-being of our planet, while also recognising that not every belief or practice is worthy of that respect. When an idea or action causes harm to individuals, communities, or the environment, it crosses a moral line. True respect is not blind tolerance; it's the willingness to honour what uplifts and protects life, and to reject what destroys or degrades it.

Real unity doesn't erase our differences. It doesn't ask anyone to give up their sacred stories or practices. Instead, it reminds us that within most spiritual and cultural paths, we share the same important principles and values.

We don't have to agree on every belief to walk together. We just need to honour the values and principles that lift us up and help us care for one another.

That is the spirit of Kairos, not blending all faiths into one, but seeing the beauty in each, and choosing to live with love, courage, and an open heart.

Chapter 2

What Is Kairos?

I never set out to create a new path. What I experienced wasn't a new set of rules or a belief system, but a change, a shift in how I saw myself, faith, and the world. It didn't happen all at once, but gradually, through questions, discoveries, and honest reflection.

Later, I came to call that shift a *Kairos* moment, a word from ancient Greek that refers not to chronological time (*chronos*), but to the right or opportune time for change. A Kairos moment is when something important becomes clear, when a truth rises to the surface, or when life invites us to move in a new direction.

Kairos isn't a religion. It's not a doctrine or a spiritual system. It's a way of recognizing those life moments that call us to pay attention, to be willing to change, to live with greater honesty, compassion, and awareness. In a world that often rushes us toward certainty and success, Kairos invites us to pause and reflect on what truly matters.

You may suddenly begin to see your life, and perhaps even the world, in a new light. A Kairos moment is like a threshold, a doorway between what was and what might be. You don't always know where it will lead, but something inside tells you it's time to take that step.

For me, Kairos is the name I give to those moments of clarity that rise up in the middle of everyday life, moments that invite change, growth, or awakening. We don't invent them, and we can't always predict them. But when they arrive, they stir something inside us. Sometimes it's during a quiet walk, a difficult conversation, or the stillness that follows a hard truth. A Kairos moment isn't loud or dramatic, but it has a way of showing us what matters most, if we're willing to listen.

These moments don't force themselves on us, and they don't try to control us, but they do invite reflection. They quietly encourage us to look within, to let go of the pressure to always be right, and to step away from systems or beliefs that may no longer feel true or helpful. Instead of clinging to what's familiar, we're invited into something more honest and freeing.

A Kairos moment helps us step out of the busyness and expectations of life and into a clearer space, a space where we can slow down, listen, and pay attention to what really matters. It offers a chance to reconnect with our inner compass, to live not just out of habit or fear, but with greater care, purpose, and openness.

In this sense, Kairos isn't just about being human in the ordinary sense. It's about becoming *more deeply human,* remembering who we are beneath all the noise, roles, and beliefs. It's about choosing to live in ways that reflect the sacred within us and around us, in how we speak, how we treat others, and how we care for the world.

Becoming deeply human isn't about being perfect. It's about being present.

Present to truth.
Present to love.
Present to life.

Why I Chose the Name

The word *Kairos* came to me slowly, like a seed that had been planted long before I understood what it was. I was looking for a word that could hold the meaning of what I had gone through, not just a change in belief, but an inner awakening. A shift that had begun quietly, yet changed everything.

I had left behind a faith that once shaped my world, and in doing so, something in me opened. I needed a word that reflected that kind of change, not a crisis or rejection, but an illumination. A turning point of the soul.

I also wanted a word that wasn't tied to one religion or tradition, but could speak across boundaries, something that could reach people from different cultures, beliefs, and experiences. I was searching for a word that could hold the quiet wisdom I had begun to sense in so many different places, in a Buddhist monk's humility, in the reverence of a Muslim's prayer, in the love of a Hindu family, in the generosity of someone with no religion at all.

I wanted to honour the deeper movement of Spirit and conscience I had come to trust, not a Spirit defined by doctrine or boxed into creeds, but one that shows up in daily life. In moments of honesty. In acts of compassion. In the still, small voice that nudges us toward love, truth, and justice.

So, I needed a word that could hold that sense of the sacred, one not claimed by a single religion, but able to speak to the soul, no matter where you come from.

When I came across *Kairos*, it felt just right.

As I mentioned earlier, in ancient Greek, it means more than time. It refers to the *right* moment, the moment of decision, the opportunity for transformation, the kind of inner timing when something real stirs and the way forward becomes clear.

It spoke not only to my personal journey but to what I sensed is happening in the world, a growing hunger for something more meaningful, more connected, and more honest.

Kairos held a sense of the sacred.
It reminded me of the quiet inner voice that nudges us to do what's right, even when it's hard.
It carried the gentle strength of a fresh beginning, not as a reaction against the past, but as a way of stepping forward with clarity and hope.

That's why I chose the name. Because *Kairos* is not just a word. It's an invitation, to live awake, to live well, and to live true.

A Sacred Shift

For some people, this shift comes gradually. Questions build. Old answers begin to feel too small. And bit by bit, a new way of seeing begins to form.

However it happens, these moments change us.

You begin to let go of what no longer fits. You start noticing how your words and actions affect others. You try to live with more honesty and kindness. Even if little changes on the outside, something inside feels different, more alive, more grounded.

This process is rarely easy.

You might lose friendships.
You might feel uncertain about who you are.
Letting go of old beliefs can feel like losing a part of yourself.

There may be times of confusion, grief, or loneliness. But inside that discomfort is a hidden gift. By releasing what no longer serves, you create space for something better: a deeper peace, a stronger sense of self, and the freedom that comes when your inner life begins to align with your outer life.

A Kairos moment isn't about joining something new. It's not about following strict rules or adopting a new label. It's a change in posture, one that grows from love, courage, and curiosity. It invites growth, healing, and a deeper connection with yourself, with others, and with what is sacred.

The Kairos Invitation

To live in Kairos is to become more present, right here, right now.

It's realizing that this moment, not tomorrow, not someday, matters. The choices we make today shape who we become and the world we create together.

Kairos invites us:

- To slow down
- To reflect

- To live with compassion and courage
- To care for others and for ourselves
- To return to what truly matters

The Kairos path is drawn from the shared wisdom of many cultures and traditions, yet it is not bound by any of them. It honors universal values like humility, integrity, love, justice, truth, and the healing power of presence.

This path isn't about perfection. It's about being honest, with yourself, with others, and with the way you live.

It doesn't mean separating from the world. It means engaging with it more deeply, recognizing how connected we all are: to each other, to the earth, and to something greater than ourselves.

And it certainly doesn't mean having all the answers.
It means staying open.
Listening.
Paying attention to what's real, both inside your heart and in the world around you.

In the next chapters, I'll explore the values and principles that shape the Kairos path, offering a way of life that seeks deeper harmony with ourselves, with others, and with the sacred.

Because once we've experienced a Kairos moment…
we can't go back.
Only forward, with open eyes and a truer heart.

Chapter 3

Principles and Values of Kairos

Now that we've explored the heart of Kairos, the moments that wake us up to deeper truths, it's time to look at the values and principles that bring those moments to life.

These aren't just ideas to believe in. They are ways of living that shape how we treat others, how we make choices, and how we face the world around us. They take the awakening of Kairos and transfer it in daily life, showing us how to walk with love, clarity, and compassion in a world that often feels divided.

Every genuine spiritual or conscious path rests on a foundation of values. These guiding principles go beyond belief, they shape how we live, how we care for others, and how we respond to the suffering we see. They grow out of reflection, compassion, and that quiet wisdom within us that whispers what is right, even when it's hard to follow.

Though ancient, these values feel more essential now than ever. In a time of conflict, confusion, and disconnection, they help us live with love, clarity, and courage.

Here are some of the values and principles at the heart of the Kairos path.

Love as the Guiding Force

The foundation of all spiritual paths. Love as empathy, service, compassion, and connection. Love that transcends fear and breaks down walls. From personal experiences and shared accounts, I've seen love radiate as both compassion and comfort. It enables positive relationships, inspires kindness, and offers solace in despair. Even those without a spiritual framework often display acts of love, suggesting a natural connection to a spiritual essence.

Love also shows itself in nature's beauty, the flutter of a Ulysses butterfly, the fragrance of a frangipani flower, or the touch of a gentle breeze. Taking time to appreciate these moments fills us with joy, gratitude, and a sense of connection to something far greater.

It is not only sentimental or romantic love, but courageous, active, and healing love, the kind that extends compassion to the stranger, seeks justice for the oppressed, and chooses connection over control.

Justice Rooted in Compassion

Justice, in the Kairos path, is not about punishment or power. It is about restoration, dignity, and fairness. It begins with compassion and ends with equity. It asks not just what is legal, but what is right, for people, for communities, and for the Earth.

At its heart, justice means making sure no one is left behind. This includes advocating for distributive justice: the fair sharing of resources, opportunities, and support, especially for those who have been excluded or exploited.

True justice goes beyond equal treatment. It creates conditions that allow each person to thrive, no matter their background or social standing.

Peace, too, is rooted in justice, not in the suppression of conflict or the use of force. True peace doesn't come from silence or fear, or from the ability to control others. It grows when people are treated fairly, when their dignity is upheld, and when their voices are heard.

In some of the countries I've lived in, peace was often spoken of, but it came at the cost of repression. The appearance of stability was maintained by silencing informed people or intimidating the poor. That kind of "peace" was more like putting a lid on a boiling pot. Eventually, the pressure builds and erupts. And in many places, it has.

Real peace must be built from the ground up. It listens to the voices of the hurting, makes space for justice, and aims not to control, but to heal.

Kairos calls us toward this deeper peace. It asks us to speak up for the voiceless, to challenge systems that harm, and to stand beside those who are striving for fairness and dignity.

One essential tool of justice is education. When people living in poverty or under oppression are given access to knowledge, skills, and resources, they gain the power to reclaim their dignity and rights.

I remember a moment in Guatemala when a wealthy local offered to show me the beautiful countryside. As we passed steep corn fields, I noticed many young people working. I asked why they weren't in school. His answer shocked me: "If they go to school and get educated, then they can rebel against us."

Thankfully, some international organizations were offering free education to poor farming families. But efforts like this must be done with care. They need wisdom and a deep understanding of local culture.

A friend of ours once worked in an Asian country where many young people were employed in garment factories under harsh conditions, low pay, long hours, and no voice to speak out. She was deeply moved by their struggles and quietly began advocating for better treatment. She helped organize small educational sessions and connected workers with a legal aid group. She wasn't loud or confrontational, just quietly determined to help them find their voice.

But one evening, without warning, she was detained by the authorities and deported. No explanation was given. Her quiet work, though rooted in compassion, had unsettled powerful interests and some name brands we commonly wear.

That experience left a lasting impression on me. It reminded me that justice requires more than passion, it also calls for wisdom. When we stand up for others, especially within systems and cultures not our own, we must listen deeply, act with care, and understand the risks involved. Good intentions are not enough; they must be guided by humility, cultural sensitivity, and thoughtful strategy.

Justice, when rooted in compassion, becomes an expression of love. It listens to the voices of the oppressed. It creates spaces where healing and fairness can grow. And above all, it remembers that justice is not about control, but about care.

This kind of justice is not confined to any one faith or region. It is a universal value. In India, a Hindu doctor gave up a successful career to open a clinic in the slums, offering care to the poor despite his family's objections. In Aleppo, Syria, Muslim clowns risked their lives to bring laughter to children during wartime. Though tragically killed, their actions showed the power of joy and compassion, even in despair.

Truth Grounded in Love and Kindness

The Kairos path invites us to search for truth, not with pride or the need to be right, but with humility and a willingness to grow. We're encouraged to hold our ideas with open hands and to keep our hearts soft, even when we feel strongly about our beliefs.

Truth is real, but rarely tidy or simple. We don't always find it in one moment or one place. It unfolds slowly, through our experiences, the people we meet, and the questions we ask. Because we're always learning, our understanding of truth deepens and changes over time.

That's why truth must be rooted in love and kindness. Without love, truth can become cold or harsh. But when shaped by love, truth becomes something that builds up rather than tears down.

Freedom with Responsibility

Kairos values spiritual freedom, the freedom to ask questions, explore new ideas, and step away from beliefs that no longer feel true. It encourages each person to follow their inner sense of what is right and good.

But freedom isn't about doing whatever we want. It's a sacred gift, and it comes with responsibility, to care for each other, to protect the Earth, and to consider how our actions affect others and future generations. Real freedom isn't just about what's best for me. It's about choosing what gives life to all.

Peace through Presence

In today's noisy world, choosing peace is a healing act. Kairos reminds us that peace begins inside us. It starts in quiet moments, when we slow down and pay attention, to what we're feeling, how we're thinking, and how we're responding to life.

Peace grows when we practice deep listening, to ourselves, to others, and to the Spirit within and around us. And it doesn't stop with inner calm. It shapes how we speak, how we handle tension, and how we treat those who are different from us.

Peace is not the absence of conflict, but the presence of gentleness and courage. It is the choice to respond with grace when it would be easier to react.

Respect for Diversity and Difference

Kairos recognizes that no single path holds all truth. Diversity is not a threat, it is a gift. We are not here to compete, convert, or correct. We are here to learn, to honor, and to grow.

That means letting go of superiority and embracing solidarity. Difference doesn't divide us, fear does. But where there is moral respect, there is room to move.

Principles of Accountability

Hold yourself and others accountable for harmful or hurtful actions. It is important to address issues promptly to prevent situations from deteriorating and to foster a culture of responsibility. Often, this involves forgiveness. Resolving issues before the day ends lifts burdens and allows us to proceed in peace. This principle extends beyond personal interactions but can also include demanding transparency from organizations, governments, corporations, and businesses.

Opposing Corruption, Lying, and Cheating

To address corruption, lying, and cheating constructively and peacefully, individuals and groups should adopt principles that promote ethical behavior, transparency, and accountability. In a world where power can corrupt, and where unethical individuals may compromise ethics, morals, and integrity, we must align our actions with the principles and values we've already listed.

The Precious Spirit – The Source of All

At the heart of Kairos is what I call the Precious Spirit. Others may know it by different names, but it is that living essence beyond ourselves, the quiet, sacred presence that moves through all of life.

This Spirit isn't tied to one religion or tradition. It can be felt in nature, in a moment of peace, in an act of kindness, or even in the voice of conscience that urges us toward compassion. It doesn't demand fear or submission; it simply calls us closer, breathing courage into weary hearts, offering strength when we feel weak, and whispering hope when we feel lost.

When we open to the Precious Spirit, we begin to notice certain qualities slowly growing within us, not imposed from the outside, but arising naturally from within.

The Fruit of the Spirit – Universal Qualities

In my earlier Christian life, I often returned to a passage called the Fruit of the Spirit. It listed qualities like:

Love, joy, peace, patience, kindness, goodness, faithfulness, gentleness, and self-control.

These qualities are not exclusive to Christianity. They are universal values, seen in people from every culture and belief. They show up wherever someone is connected to something greater than themselves.

To this list, I would add:
- Wisdom – the ability to see clearly and choose wisely
- Knowledge – gaining knowledge in or to know
- Understanding – the willingness to truly listen and connect
- The power to overcome – inner strength to endure hardship with grace

These are not traits to show off, they are qualities we grow over time, through reflection, humility, and connection to Spirit.

These Are Not Just Virtues, They Are Practices

The principles and values of Kairos are not rules to control you. They are reminders, gentle guideposts when the world feels heavy.

They are not fixed answers, but anchors you can return to. They are not here to force belief, but to invite deeper living:

- One that honors life.
- One that honors moral differences.
- One that trusts in the quiet wisdom already growing inside you, and inside others.

Following the Kairos path isn't just about believing these values. It's about practicing them, as best we can, day by day, even when it's hard. It's about abiding in them, and returning to them when we lose our way.

They become the light we carry through dark times, the compass we trust when we've stepped away from rigid dogmas but still long for direction.

What matters most is not how much we know, but how deeply we care, and how we choose to live in the time we've been given.

Chapter 4

The Inner Shift

From Awakening to Action

A Note on the Word "Spirituality"

The word spirituality can mean many things. For some, it's a source of comfort and purpose. For others, especially those who've stepped away from religion, it may carry baggage, feel unclear, or seem tied to beliefs they no longer hold.

When I use the word here, I don't mean a set of doctrines or a belief system. I mean something deeper and more human: the way we search for meaning, live with awareness, act with love, and stay connected to what feels true.

You might call it your inner life, your conscience, your soul, sacred awareness, or simply your truest self. Whatever name fits for you, this chapter is an invitation to explore that deeper part of life in a way that's personal, honest, and healing.

Not everyone sees themselves as religious. Some have left the traditions they were raised in. Others were never part of one. Yet many still speak of moments that feel deeply meaningful, times of stillness, beauty, love, or connection to something greater than themselves.

To me, this is the heart of the inner shift. It's not about doctrine or belief systems, it's about how we engage with life. How we show up, how we treat others, how deeply we listen.

It's not just what we believe, but how we live.

This shift invites us to:

- Live with care, by being kind, thoughtful, and attentive.
- Live with depth, by looking beneath the surface to what really matters.
- Live with presence, by being here, awake, not just following routines or systems.
- Live with integrity, by aligning our actions with our values, even when it's hard.

Why This Inner Life Still Matters

Many people today feel disillusioned with religion, but that doesn't mean they've lost the longing for meaning.

They still want purpose.
They still seek connection.
They still hope for something true.

They're not looking for more rules. They're looking for something real.

They want:

- A kind of meaning that honours their questions, respects their intelligence, and speaks to both the heart and the mind.
- Connection and community without control or obligation.
- A sense of wonder that awakens us, not rules that restrain us.

What they're really searching for isn't religion, it's a deeper, more honest way of being.

This kind of life welcomes questions. It grows not from fear, but from love and conscience.
It can be found inside some traditions, and also far outside of them.
In the end, it's not about what label you wear. It's about how you live.

From Beliefs to Experience

One of the most freeing discoveries on my journey was this:
I didn't need to have all the answers to feel at peace.

For years, I clung to fixed beliefs, needing certainty. But when I stepped beyond those systems, I discovered something quieter and deeper: direct experience.

It's what happens when:

- You sit in silence and feel something greater nearby.
- You walk in nature and are filled with awe.

- You show kindness to someone in pain and feel your own heart open.
- You witness suffering and respond, not with fear, but with compassion.

These moments aren't just emotional.
They are sacred.
They are signs of the inner shift taking root.

When Borders Fall

Letting go of religious borders didn't make my world smaller.
It made it wider, richer.

I began to learn from other traditions, not to replace my path, but to receive wisdom.
I no longer needed to defend a single "right" way.
I could listen with humility and let truth speak in many voices.

The Spirit, or call it love, or presence, or truth, moves where it will. Through dreams, through music, through strangers, through silence. Even through doubt.

We're not here to control the sacred. We're here to stay open to it.

A Path That Heals

The inner shift is not the end of a journey. It's the beginning of a deeper responsibility.

The Kairos path invites us to grow, not just for ourselves, but for the sake of others, for our communities, and for the Earth.

We're not only here to evolve inwardly. We're here to help heal what's broken.

To walk this path means seeing the world not only as it is, but as it could be, and doing our part to help shape it.

It means becoming a presence of kindness where others might withdraw.
Speaking with more gentleness.
Listening more deeply.
Acting with intention, not because we're perfect, but because we care enough to try.

I'm still learning, too.

The Power of Attention

One of the most powerful things we can do is what I call spiritual attention, the quiet act of turning your heart toward someone or something in need, with love and intention.

This might mean:

- Holding someone in quiet thought speaking positive affirmations

- Calling on the Spirit to move upon a person's needs, even a leader in a hard moment

- Mentally sending illumination and compassion toward someone who's caused harm, hoping they awaken

This isn't about controlling outcomes.
It's about being a vessel for healing.
A channel through which the Spirit, or love, or light, can move.

Sometimes I simply whisper:
Spirit, be near. Be present. Be light.
Then I let go.

Even when we can't see the results, I believe these moments plant invisible seeds.
The Spirit will water them in its own time.

A Movement the World Needs

The world is aching.

We face war, greed, climate breakdown, and a deep loss of truth and connection.
These are not only political or economic problems.
They are spiritual problems, signs of our disconnection from love, from each other, and from the sacredness of life.

What the world needs now isn't more ideology or control.
It needs a new kind of awareness, a deeper way of living.

Imagine if people from all walks of life, religious or not, chose to:

- Live with courage, integrity and compassion

- Act justly, even when it costs something

- Honour and respect the Earth and all life

- Pause and reflect before reacting

- Forgive others and ourselves

- Be peacemakers, healers, and voices of dignity

This isn't naïve thinking. It's a deep, grounded hope.

When enough people live with love and awareness, the world begins to shift.

A Call to You

I don't offer this as a rulebook, but as a vision.
Not as something to believe, but something to consider.

If you've ever felt that the world is aching for something deeper…
If you've longed to be part of something that heals rather than harms…
If you've wondered whether your quiet, inner life could help shape the outer world…

Then I believe this may be your **Kairos** moment.

Not the only one, but maybe the one that matters most right now.

You are not alone.
You are not powerless.
You are not too late.

The Spirit is near.
The time is now.
And the path, though not easy, is open.

Chapter 5

Navigating Harmful Beliefs and Practices

Coming out of the last chapter, where we explored how the inner shift of Kairos moves us from awakening to action, there's an important question we can't ignore:

How do we navigate the beliefs and practices around us, especially the ones that might cause harm?

When I first began sharing the ideas in this book, my daughter once asked me, with quiet honesty,
"Can people really come together across such deep divides?"

Her question stayed with me.

The truth is, not every belief or tradition leads to love, kindness, or freedom. Some ideas, even when called "spiritual," can still cause harm. While Kairos invites us to be open-minded and respectful, it also reminds us to stay wise. Real unity grows when there's a shared foundation of kindness, fairness, and truth.

Kairos isn't about believing the same things. It's about living from shared values, what I call the **common ground.** These include love, light, life, justice, care for the Earth, and the timeless qualities mentioned earlier as the Fruit of the Spirit:

love, joy, peace, patience, kindness, goodness, faithfulness, gentleness, and self-control.

Added to these are values like truth, humility, compassion, and presence, the kind of presence that listens and cares. These are not just nice words. They're everyday guides. They help us recognize what builds up and what tears down.

Staying Open Without Losing Ourselves

Living from Kairos means staying open, to people, ideas, cultures, and stories. Wisdom can come from many places, and we're called to listen with humility.

But being open doesn't mean accepting everything.

It's not loving to stay silent when people are being hurt. It's not kind to ignore abuse or injustice just to "keep the peace."

True openness has boundaries.

It listens with respect but also speaks up with courage. Walking the Kairos path means holding two things together:

- Humility to learn from others, and
- Courage to say no to what causes harm.

Seeing Through Harmful Systems

During my years living and working in other countries, I encountered many beautiful traditions, but I also witnessed belief systems that created fear, guilt, or control.

I saw people told their worth depended on blind obedience.
I saw communities where women, children, or the poor were silenced or exploited.

Kairos doesn't give us a rigid rulebook; it gives us a **compass**.

A way to sense whether something leads to wholeness, or to harm.

Here are some questions we can ask when we encounter a belief or practice:

- Does it bring peace, or fear?
- Does it build people up, or break them down?
- Does it honor life, or take away dignity?
- Does it care for the Earth, or exploit it?

These questions can guide us, whether we're part of a faith community, exploring alone, or navigating unfamiliar traditions.

Naming the Most Harmful Expressions

Sadly, there are belief systems and movements that go far beyond harmless differences, they cause deep harm.

- **Fundamentalist Sects:** Some twist faith into control, creating closed communities that oppress individuals, especially women, and reject diversity.
- **Religious Nationalist Movements:** These merge faith with politics, using "divine authority" as an excuse for exclusion, persecution, or violence.

- **Prosperity Teachings:** These equate wealth with divine favor, turning spirituality into a transaction and often leaving followers in financial and emotional ruin.
- **Totalitarian Religious Movements:** These justify terror or violence under the guise of spiritual purification, using fear to dominate and divide.

These examples remind us why boundaries matter. They show what happens when spirituality is used for power, control, or personal gain, straying far from love and integrity.

In contrast, Kairos seeks a global community that embraces diversity, upholds dignity, and promotes peaceful, ethical living grounded in love.

Shared Integrity, Not Shared Belief

The Kairos path isn't about uniformity. It doesn't demand everyone use the same words or agree on every practice.

What matters most is **shared integrity.**

This means:

- Living honestly and responsibly.
- Choosing kindness, not as a rule, but as a way of being.
- Showing respect, even when we disagree.

Integrity doesn't require sameness. It asks for alignment with love, truth, and conscience.

When people walk together with this kind of integrity, a spiritual community can take shape that doesn't depend on conformity. We don't have to erase our differences to build something meaningful.

A Final Thought

Kairos isn't here to replace anyone's faith.

It's here to nurture what is true and loving, wherever that is found.

But if any belief or practice begins to drift away from compassion, dignity, or care for others, Kairos invites us to pause.

To come back to what matters.
To let love, humility, and truth guide the way again.

So let us stay open.
Let us stay grounded.
And let us walk forward,
With love.
With courage.
With humility.
And with clarity.

Chapter 6

Which One Is the One True Belief?

Before we finish this first part of the book, I want to pause and reflect on a question that has followed me for much of my former Christian life. It shaped my thinking, challenged my beliefs, and slowly led me toward a different way of seeing.

The question is this:
Is there such a thing as "the one true belief/religion"?

I asked it quietly in my own heart, and sometimes aloud in conversations, especially as I met people from many cultures, faiths, and life stories. I carried it through years of devotion, doubt, searching, and discovery.

What I found didn't lead me to one final answer. It led me to a doorway, a new way of understanding faith and spirituality that is broader, more compassionate, and grounded in our shared humanity.

And it changed everything.

Searching for Truth

For hundreds of years, people have debated what makes a religion "true." Some say it's the number of followers. Others point to a religion's history, its miracles, or its sacred texts. Some focus on moral teachings, wondering whether a religion inspires people to live with goodness and integrity.

But when we look honestly at the world, we see that no religion has been perfect.

Christianity, Islam, Hinduism, Buddhism, all of them have brought wisdom, beauty, and hope into people's lives. But all of them have also, at times, caused harm. Wars, oppression, exclusion, and fear have sometimes been carried out in the name of religion.

If we're searching for the one religion that has never failed, that has never harmed anyone, that holds all truth and light perfectly, we won't find it.

Maybe we're asking the wrong question.

Instead of asking: *Which religion is the only true one?*
Maybe we should be asking: *What kind of path leads us toward love, truth, and healing?*

A Deeper Realization

After many years of living in different cultures, serving as a missionary, and learning from people of many faiths, I came to a clear realization:

There is no single path that owns the whole truth.
No one group holds all the answers.
The sacred is not confined to one religion.

What I came to believe, and what Kairos affirms, is that beneath all our differences in belief, language, and ritual, there is a shared spiritual essence. A common thread that runs through all true expressions of the sacred.

Some call this the Universal Spirit, the Divine Presence, God, Source, Life, or simply Love.

Whatever name we use, the essence is the same: a presence of love, connection, and wisdom that moves through life itself.

It is not owned by any one religion. It is bigger than any system or label. It shows up in many forms, across cultures and generations.

What This Means for Faith

As I've shared earlier, my years as a missionary across Southeast Asia exposed me to countless people, Muslims, Buddhists, Hindus, Christians, and those following traditional or Indigenous practices.

Many of them did not share my beliefs. But they lived with deep kindness, generosity, and respect for life.

They were not "lost."
They were not less valuable because they didn't believe what I believed.

They were already walking with the sacred, in their own way.

This changed me.

I began to see that while our outer forms may differ, our prayers, rituals, and sacred texts, many of the core values are the same:

- Love
- Compassion
- Kindness
- Justice
- Integrity
- Humility
- Respect for life

These are the fruits of the Spirit, and they are not limited to any one religion. They are universal.

When Certainty Hurts

Sadly, when people believe their religion is the only true one, it often leads to harm.

I've seen this firsthand. I've lived it.

When my wife and I became missionaries, we were sure we were doing the right thing. We believed our version of Christianity was the truth, and we acted with conviction. But we didn't fully see the pain our certainty caused, especially for loved ones who didn't share our beliefs.

It wasn't until years later, when we began stepping away from those rigid ideas, that we could see the damage it had done. Since then, we've worked to repair those relationships and walk a more open, compassionate path.

A Way That Unites, Not Divides

Kairos doesn't ask anyone to abandon their faith or to adopt a new label.

As we've explored in this book, it's not a religion, it's a way of seeing. A reminder that the sacred isn't confined to one group.

Kairos invites us to look for the qualities that matter most:

- Does this path lead to love?
- Does it encourage kindness and justice?
- Does it honor the sacredness of life?
- Does it build bridges rather than walls?

If it does, then it's a path worth walking.
If it doesn't, it may be time to let it go.

Honouring Our Moral Differences

Today, the world is home to over 4,000 religions, and countless ways of living spiritually. That's not a problem, it's a gift.

Each path carries its own wisdom, its own stories, its own beauty.

Some beliefs will need to be questioned, especially when they harm others. But the human longing for meaning, connection, and truth is something we all share.

Kairos calls us beyond the need to be right, into the desire to be whole.

It's not about what we call our beliefs. It's about how we live them.

It's not about having the final answer. It's about continuing the journey, with open eyes and an open heart.

Walking Forward Together

Let us honor the richness of our differences, and at the same time, hold onto the thread that connects us all:
The Universal Spirit, the sacred presence that lives within and beyond all things.

This is the path I walk now. A path that welcomes people from all backgrounds.

A path that values love, courage, humility, and compassion.

A path that doesn't require us to all agree, but invites us to live with honesty and heart.

Let us walk forward,
Not divided by dogma, but united by love.
Not bound by fear, but opened by trust.
Not trying to convert the world, but choosing to care for it.

Closing Part One

This brings us to the end of Part One, the heart and vision of Kairos.

In Part Two, I'll share the journey that brought me here:

The years I spent deeply involved in Christianity.
The strong desire I had to serve others, and the cost that came with it.
The slow unraveling of beliefs I once held tightly.

And the discovery of a more open, honest, and loving way of seeing life, culture, and the sacred.

Part 2

The Journey That Led Me Here

Everything shared in Part 1, the values, the vision, and the spirit of Kairos, didn't come to me overnight. They were born out of real experiences: years of faith, deep questions, surprising discoveries, and quiet moments of awakening.

In the next chapters, I want to take you behind the vision, into the life that shaped it. This is the story of how I came to the edge of what I once believed, and how, in one quiet morning in Yangon, the turning point finally arrived.

So now we begin Part 2, a path shaped by faith, change, loss, questions, and finally, awakening.

Chapter 7

The Turning Point: A Morning in Yangon

This next part isn't written to convince you of anything.
It's simply here to share my story.
Not to preach, but to reflect.
Not to give you the answers, but to offer a mirror.
So that maybe, in the ups and downs of my journey, you might recognize parts of your own.
We all walk different paths. But sometimes, hearing someone else's story helps us understand our own more clearly.

It was in Yangon, Myanmar, that I left behind the religion of Christianity. That decision opened the door to deeper reflection, new discoveries, and a more open, less judgmental outlook toward people of other faiths and beliefs.

In 2013, on a warm, humid morning, I found myself at a Christian Men's Breakfast in Yangon. The room smelled faintly of coffee and fried eggs. The AC's fanned the room, struggling to cut through the humid air. Around the tables, men in polo shirts and button-downs talked quietly as plates clinked and coffee cups became empty. I had been invited to speak about my early missionary experiences to a group of expatriate men, missionaries, and local leaders gathered for food, fellowship, and testimonies.

It was meant to be a simple, half-hour talk. But as I neared the end, I felt something rising in me, a strong, undeniable pull to share the shift I had been carrying quietly for years. My heart was pounding. I knew that what I was about to say would distance me from a world I had belonged to for decades. But I also knew I couldn't keep it in any longer.

The Long Unfolding

The process leading to this moment had been building for a long time. I had wrestled with growing uncertainty about core elements of my Christian faith, questioning the very foundations of doctrines I once took for granted.

One pressing question weighed heavily on me: *Is Christianity truly the only way to connect with God, the one exclusive path to salvation through Jesus?* This led to another question, *"What about the countless people who lived before Jesus, or those who never had a chance to hear his name?"*

My 12 years of missionary work across five Asian countries had given me deep friendships with people of many faiths, Muslims, Buddhists, Hindus, and with others who had no religious label at all. The more I loved and respected these friends, the harder it became to believe that they might be condemned simply because they didn't follow Jesus.

By 2011, I knew I had to reevaluate everything I believed. I studied, reflected, and asked hard questions, helped by former Christian scholars who approached it with honesty and scholarship. Stories like Jonah's three days inside a large fish, Adam and Eve's talking serpent, or the donkey that spoke, I began to see them less as literal history and more as metaphors carrying deeper lessons.

I questioned whether the Bible was the "absolute word of God," whether Jesus' resurrection was literal, and whether the many miracles attributed to him were historical or symbolic. Walking on water. Turning water into wine. Feeding thousands from a few loaves and fish. These stories seemed intended to magnify his greatness, but were they meant to be taken literally?

These doubts didn't come in one sudden burst; they grew slowly, one question after another, until I could no longer ignore them.

Slowly, a different picture emerged, and many of the old answers no longer fit. I began slowly stepping away from Christianity, not with bitterness or anger, but with honesty and peace. I honoured what the faith had given me: purpose, meaning, language for love, and a global sense of community.

But I could no longer live within its doctrinal walls.

I still believed in Jesus, the man Jesus, his compassion, his justice, his example of radical love. But I no longer believed in a transactional gospel built on blood sacrifice. I no longer saw "sin" as a stain that required cleansing, but rather as a disconnection from love and harmony that needed to be healed.

And I no longer believed that Christianity had exclusive access to spiritual truth.

Speaking the Truth Aloud

So, that morning in Yangon, when I stood before that group, I made a choice: I would speak the truth that had been stirring in me for so long.

I took a breath and said:

"I no longer believe that salvation or a connection to God is found only through faith in Jesus Christ. And I no longer believe that he bodily resurrected from the dead. He was an incredible man, deeply close to the spirit."

The room went silent, a quiet shocked silence. The silence stretched, before a few hesitant voices finally broke it. Then came a wave of questions, some curious, others defensive. I did my best to respond calmly, but the energy in the room had changed. Thankfully, the meeting had a time limit, and it soon drew to a close.

I walked out into the bright, humid air feeling two things at once: a sting from the shock and discomfort I had caused, and a strange, unmistakable freedom. For the first time, I had said aloud what I truly believed and, in that honesty, I felt a weight lift.

One man approached me privately afterward and said, "I've had similar doubts... but I've never had the courage to say them out loud." That simple admission touched me deeply. It reminded me that I wasn't alone, and that maybe, just maybe, someone else needed to hear my words.

I went home that day feeling lighter, freer, more whole than I had felt in years.

That moment was my Kairos, not just a crisis, but a sacred turning point. A change in the timeline of my belief. A moment when Spirit whispered, *"You are free to go."*

It Was Freeing

Not everyone welcomed these changes. Some Christian friends and colleagues responded with unease, even quiet disappointment. Though I attended the International Church for a while longer, the tension of conflicting beliefs, and the growing isolation as word of my shift spread, eventually led me to stop going altogether.

Debbie, thankfully, remained a steady presence, supportive even as she held on to some of her own Christian beliefs. In time, we found a new circle of friends, many non-religious, within the international community. Our weekends filled with countryside explorations and visits to Buddhist temples with colleagues, who explained the symbols and paintings with warmth and pride. I didn't feel the need to convert anyone or "save their souls." I just received their hospitality, their sincerity, and their deep cultural wisdom.

It was incredibly freeing.

I began to see the world through wider eyes. Spirituality, I realized, whether called God, The Source, The Ground of Being, The Universe, or The Cosmos, is not the property of one religion. It is the shared thread that weaves through all traditions, allowing us to respect each one's beauty without demanding they all be the same.

I didn't stop being spiritual. In fact, I was becoming spiritual in a new way, one that didn't demand certainty or exclusivity. I began to study different aspects of Spirituality and meditation. I read books and listened to stories from others who had walked a similar path, former Christians still connected to the Sacred in meaningful, evolving ways.

A New Beginning

Myanmar marked the end of one spiritual era, and the beginning of another. I had said the words. I had finally exposed my hidden secret and it was so freeing. And I was no longer afraid. The path ahead was uncertain. But I looked forward to it.

To understand how I got there, we need to go back, to my earliest memories of faith, the childhood beliefs that shaped me, and the first stirrings of wonder that long preceded any theology

Chapter 8

A Religious Childhood and My Exploring Nature

My life's journey has been shaped by both adversity and wonder, by painful discipline and awe-inspiring freedom. The challenges I faced, even from a young age, forged in me a deep resilience, a reflective mind, and a sense of curiosity that would one day take me across the world. I've come to see that these early experiences, some joyful, some harsh, became the soil in which my questioning spirit and spiritual search would grow.

I was born in 1951 in Hamilton, Ontario, Canada, a bustling city known for its steel industry, nestled between Toronto and Niagara Falls. My father worked in one of the city's massive steel refineries. He was a quiet man but deeply passionate about gardening and archaeology, two interests that subtly shaped my own outlook. I can still remember the tidy rows in the garden, and the calm with which he would explain his fascination with ancient civilizations. He also painted landscapes during the snowy winters, capturing the stillness and beauty of rural landscapes. Some of that creative spark, I believe, has carried on in my daughters and grandchildren.

My mother, Ursula, left when I was just two years old, and much of my early childhood was spent in daycare or under the stern watch of a caregiver.

After my parents divorced, my father married Gabriela, a no-nonsense nurse who brought strict order into our home. We lived in a gritty neighborhood, across from a wholesale beer distributor and near noisy train tracks. It wasn't idyllic by any stretch, but it was what we had. I walked nearly 3 kilometers to school each day, my arm heavy with books. There was even a time I was attacked by a stray dog on my route, which left a lasting impression. Still, this was the expected rhythm of life.

At home, I was often occupied with chores, shoveling snow, weeding the garden, but when I had free time, I found great joy in exploring the woods nearby. Nature became my quiet refuge. I was drawn to birdwatching, collecting and identifying leaves, and building forts with friends. I also loved taking apart gadgets to see how they worked, then trying, often unsuccessfully, to put them back together. This mixture of creativity, solitude, and curiosity became a core part of who I was. Looking back, I see those quiet hours in nature as some of my first true spiritual experiences, though I would not have called them that at the time.

Early Religious Impressions

Spiritually, my early life was grounded in Roman Catholicism. We attended church regularly, and I was enrolled in a Catholic school situated right next to our parish. I served as an altar boy, more mischievous than holy, and on occasion, my fellow altar servers and I would sneak sips of communion wine in the vestry. The God I was introduced to was stern and watchful, a cosmic judge keeping tabs on my every sin. I prayed often, especially after confessing my wrongdoings to the priest, and the recited penance prayers became a form of psychological reset, helping me feel clean again.

One film had deeply affected my early spiritual imagination. It featured a boy who snuck up to his attic and then confided in a statue of Jesus on a cross. The statue would eventually come to life to comfort him. That simple story moved me deeply. I related to that boy. I often visited the church alone in the evenings, pretending I was going for a run, and lit candles, and sat near a statue of Jesus, quietly whispering my hopes and sorrows. Though the statue never moved or spoke, those moments made me feel seen and calm.

My understanding of Jesus was fragmented. I knew he had been crucified, that he stood for love and forgiveness, but the details escaped me. The Virgin Mary, too, was a distant figure, I knew she was important, but I didn't feel a connection. I sometimes prayed to her but never sensed a response. Still, Catholicism gave me my first moral compass. It taught me about good and bad, reward and punishment. And perhaps more importantly, it sparked my earliest questions: After repeatedly praying for help at school, why haven't my grades improved that much?

Life at home was often tense. My stepmother was harsh, especially when it came to academic performance. If I did not meet expectations, the consequences were severe, sometimes physical. My half-brother received similar treatment, though I bore the brunt of it. At age 12, after a particularly rough period of fear and a low percentage report card, I ran away from home. I walked 12 kilometers to the Dundas train station, dreaming of hopping a train westward like I had seen on TV. I waited in the cold for hours before finally turning back. Oddly, that experience seemed to shift something in the household, afterward, the punishments became less frequent.

Not all of childhood was harsh. Some of my warmest memories involve my Aunt Cilly, who offered a refuge of love and kindness. Her home was filled with the smell of baked plum cakes and chocolate marble cake. When we visited, I felt safe, fed, and wanted. She gave me something vital, affection without conditions. Her presence was like a candle in the dark.

As I moved into adolescence, sports such as soccer, water polo and lacrosse, became a lifeline. They offered a way to escape the tension at home and connect with peers.

Chapter 9

Leaving Home, Seeking Life

By the time I was sixteen, I had had enough. I left home altogether and moved into a friend's gloomy and cold basement. Soon after, I found work with an underground mining company in Sudbury. I was too light for the job, so I hid lead weights in my winter coat to meet the minimum weight requirement. The work was brutal, and the men around me were rough, but I kept my head down and stayed out of trouble.

Eventually, after saving enough money, and weary of the monotonous routine, I hitchhiked west to Calgary, Alberta. Living on a shoestring budget, I rented a spartan room where I cooked hotdogs, beans, and buns on an oil heater for sustenance. Financial desperation led me to occasionally steal food to make ends meet. My circumstances improved when I secured a job with an oil exploration company in Northern Alberta. It was a grueling experience of intense, cold demanding work. Despite the negative after-hours activities at the work camp, I managed to avoid getting involved. Yet through it all, I felt myself growing stronger, not just physically, but mentally and emotionally.

College and a Devastating Setback

After that contract I enrolled in a small college in Calgary, Alberta, trying to build a different future and hoping to get a few more credentials under my belt. It was a hope-filled move, but it didn't last.

After eight months into the program, a trusted professor tried to molest me during a private meeting in his office. I managed to break free, unlock the door and ran with a fear driven energy out of the building and down the street. I was shaken, confused, and uncertain how to respond. At that time, such incidents were rarely reported or understood. I withdrew from the college shortly after. The financial strain was heavy because I hadn't completed the course, so once again I was in search for an income.

It was a frightening experience, but it also made something clear: I needed to keep moving forward, no matter what.

A Growing Discomfort with the System

Somewhere in this time of hardship and wandering, a new awareness began to take shape. My perspective on capitalism with its focus on profit over people, shifted significantly as I began to develop a deeper awareness of the inequalities in the world. This realization led me to take a more critical view of mainstream institutions and corporations.

I didn't have the words for it then, but I began to sense that the system we lived in was imbalanced, geared toward exploitation rather than human dignity. It sparked the first flickers of what would become a lifelong questioning of greed-based structures, something that would later become part of the ethical foundations of *Kairos*.

By this time, my long hair and unconventional thinking earned me the label of "hippie." But what others saw as rebellion was, for me, an awakening, a quiet refusal to fit into a mold that no longer made sense.

These years laid the groundwork for everything that followed: the questioning, the seeking, the eventual letting go of rigid systems of belief. But they also planted the seeds of wonder, reverence for nature, a hunger for truth, and the courage to challenge what didn't feel right.

All of this, my early religious experiences, my time in nature, my family struggles, and the raw independence of my youth, became the foundation of the spiritual path I now call Kairos. Not a path away from truth, but a path toward a deeper one.

And this, as you'll see, was just the beginning.

A Life-Changing Meeting

Then, something beautiful happened.

While working as a cook in Banff, Alberta, I met a remarkable young woman, who worked in the China Shop at the grand Banff Springs Hotel. Her warmth, energy, and kindness were disarming. She didn't just tolerate my rough edges, she softened them.

That woman, Debb, would become my wife.

Together, we embraced the wilderness around us. We hiked, climbed, biked, and canoed through the stunning Rockies, drinking in the beauty of the natural world. Those days, immersed in nature, rekindled from my childhood that inner joy, of being close to what I still called Mother Nature that connection, presence, and simplicity.

Forests Over Fine Dining

Leaving Banff as a couple, our journey took us to Victoria, British Columbia, where I decided to try working the upper-class lifestyle, as a waiter in an upscale restaurant, complete with a tuxedo. Unfortunately, this stint was short-lived. Just a few months in, I accidentally spilled red wine on the very revealing white dress of a wealthy customer. Her husband responded by leaving me with a mere five-cent tip.

We headed north west, this time to Long Beach on Vancouver Island, where we lived in a coastal house with a wood-fired sauna and the Pacific Ocean at our doorstep. I worked on the highways, and Debb waitressed at the Wickaninnish Lodge. We'd heat the sauna until it was blazing, then plunge into the frigid sea, rituals of cleansing, laughter, and renewal.

Then came Whistler. I built ski chalets to mid-day and skied on the slopes in the afternoon. Debb sold lift tickets. We almost bought a vacant block of land for $5,800, but the real estate agent wasn't in his office on that particular day. So we gave up the idea. Today, that same lot is worth hundreds of thousands.

Regrets didn't stay long. We were alive, in love, and moving forward.

In these years of trial and discovery, something deeper was forming. I wasn't yet religious. But I had begun to live with spiritual questions, about meaning, injustice, beauty, and the purpose of it all.

And though I didn't know it yet, another turning point was coming, one that would pull me into faith, mission, and eventually, into a profound spiritual reckoning.

Chapter 10

Turning Toward Faith

By the time Debb and I had settled in Whistler, I was no longer running from life. I was beginning to build one, shaped by sweat, survival, wilderness, and love.

I had known the rigid Catholicism of my youth and left it behind, but the desire for something sacred had never quite gone away. It had simply been hidden. Now, with life slowing and roots beginning to grow, that desire resurfaced, not in crisis, but in curiosity. At this stage in my spiritual journey, I began to equate Mother Nature with God. While I didn't follow any organized religion, the strong moral principles instilled in me during my early life remained a guiding force.

It was during this time that Debb moved back to Ontario, and she enrolled at the University of Toronto. Our relationship had gone through a bit of a rocky season. I spent the next few months traveling through Europe, Germany, France, the Netherlands, hoping to find clarity and something of myself. While in Germany I reunited with my parents which brought healing to our relationship.

When I returned to Canada, I met Debbie at the Toronto airport with a bouquet of tulips, and something in both of us softened.

That moment marked a quiet recommitment, not just to each other, but to walking a path together, whatever shape it might take.

A New Kind of Christianity

While Debbie was finishing her degree I moved to Peterborough, Ontario, where I enrolled at Trent University as a mature student. In the midst of this academic chapter of my life, in 1976, Debbie and I celebrated our union through a potluck wedding in Peterborough, Ontario.

Not too long after our wedding, something unexpected happened: I met a young couple whose faith was somewhat different from my understanding of Christianity. They introduced me to Protestant Christianity that was unlike anything I'd known growing up. Their words were simple but sincere. They spoke of Jesus as not just a distant figure on a cross, but as someone who could be known, personally, directly, intimately. They believed that eternal life and spiritual truth came only through Jesus, and though that exclusivity troubled me at first, their sincerity and warmth softened my resistance. I asked many questions and over time, something began to shift. I began to embrace this new form of Christianity, not because I fully understood it, but because it satisfied a silent longing I had for years. It offered a sense of purpose, belonging, community and spiritual clarity. And most powerfully, it gave me language for things I had felt my whole life but didn't known how to express.

Debb joined me in exploring this new faith. A year later, she, too, embraced this understanding of Jesus, not out of pressure, but from her own place of reflection and conviction.

Searching for the True Way

In 1979, we left Peterborough, Ontario, and headed west to Calgary, Alberta. There, my wife Debb taught at a college and I worked as a carpenter. It was in Calgary that I explored a few other religions but found certain aspects troubling. One religion believed that its adherents ascended to the highest level of heaven, while the rest of humanity remained below them. Another prohibited the consumption of meat with blood and taught that only 144,000 of its followers would reach their version of paradise. At that time in my life, I felt my version of spirituality made more sense and was quite easy to follow. It emphasized personal relationship, forgiveness, and transformation. It felt like a spiritual home we could build our lives around.

We were ready to settle in, to grow deeper, and to serve with purpose.

Building a Sanctuary

Not long after, we bought a 20-hectare block of land near Tête Jaune in the Rocky Mountains of British Columbia. We built a log-and-wood-frame house with our own hands, raised goats and honeybees, planted organic gardens, and began to live a kind of self-sufficient life that felt both deeply spiritual and deeply human.

In that quiet sanctuary, we welcomed our first two daughters into the world. The land became not just a home, but a special place as it was alive, peaceful, and filled with love.

We also found a faith community, an Apostolic Christian church in the nearby town of Valemount. There, we felt seen, supported, and strengthened. We sang hymns, read Scripture, and began to form our spiritual identity around service, and what we felt was truth.

It was an era of joy, commitment, and spiritual passion. We truly believed we had found the way, and we wanted to share it.

But there was more ahead.

Because during one church service, a visiting missionary challenged us:

"Will you go and preach this Gospel to the nations?"

That call landed deep. We had always believed that real faith must be lived, not just spoken. And this felt like the next step.

We didn't know it then, but that choice, to say yes, would shape the next fourteen years of our lives. Years that would lead us across continents, through immense sacrifice, and eventually, through the unraveling of everything we once held as absolute.

Chapter 11

The Missionary Years Begin

A visiting missionary stood before our small congregation and spoke with passion:

"The Gospel is not meant to be hoarded. Who will go? Who will carry it to the nations?"

Something in me stirred. It wasn't guilt or pressure. It was a calling, a deep sense that we were meant to take this faith we now embraced and give it away, to serve others in places where resources were few and hope was scarce.

The timing felt right. We were young, able-bodied, spiritually energized, and ready to make sacrifices. We had already left so much behind, why not keep going? Why not give everything?

And so, in 1981, I left my work in forestry, we rented out our beloved hobby farm, and I enrolled in Bible College in Caroline, Alberta.

It felt like obedience.
It felt like trust.
It felt like the next chapter of a life wholly given to God.

Training for the Field

Bible College deepened my understanding of Scripture and the evangelical worldview. But I quickly realized that theology alone wouldn't be enough. If we were going to serve in developing nations, we needed practical training, tools that could truly help people.

So we moved to Cambridge, Ontario, where we joined a Discipleship Training School through Youth With A Mission (YWAM). It was our first taste of international ministry. As part of the course, we traveled to Belize and Guatemala, working in poor communities and learning to serve with humility.

Next, we enrolled in a Long-Range Community Development course in Tacoma, Washington, which took us to Haiti and the Dominican Republic. The conditions were difficult, the lessons real. I contracted Typhoid Fever during that time and faced a stark reckoning. Lying fevered and weak, I thought:

If I die, let it be in service to something greater than myself.

Thankfully, I recovered, but the moment stayed with me.

To complete our preparation, I enrolled in two more programs at William Carey University in California, one in International Development, and the other in Primary Health Care. At that point, we had added a third daughter to our growing family.

The vision was clear: live simply, serve fully, and present the message faithfully.

A New Life Begins – Pakistan

In 1985, after years of preparation, we were commissioned and set out for Pakistan. Our daughters were just 3, 6, and 7 years old. We arrived as a family of five, full of conviction, calling, and idealism.

We weren't going as "missionaries" in the formal sense. Our visa title was Development Workers, a designation that allowed us to operate openly in a complex and often sensitive region. Our early work focused on Afghan refugees and later in communities in the Hunza Valley, in the mountainous north.

It was hard work, but I fully enjoyed it. We built relationships, distributed supplies, and worked on tangible projects such as:

- A cemented sewage drainage ditch and capping a spring in the refugee camps
- A water sand filtration system in Hunza
- A shelter to dry apples and apricots to support local livelihoods

But even as we gave, we received.
The Pakistani people and the Afghan refugees, both, were often generous, gracious, and curious. They opened their homes and their hearts to us.

Life as a Family on the Field

Not everyone in our extended family understood our decision to move overseas.

Our parents, especially, found it difficult. They were proud of our values but deeply worried about the risks, worried most of all for the children. To them, raising a young family in Pakistan seemed unsafe, even irresponsible. To them, we had stepped outside of what made sense.

To us, it felt entirely natural. We weren't driven by pressure or guilt. We didn't feel crushed by a sense of being "called." We felt at home in the places we lived. We respected the communities around us, and our thinking was straightforward: "If the people here can live and thrive in these conditions, then so can we."

Life wasn't without its challenges, of course.

One holiday, we returned to find our home completely robbed, literally everything was taken except for our sleeping mattresses. We were reminded that living in solidarity as western foreigners meant living with vulnerability, too.

Travel through the mountain regions of northern Pakistan was terrifying at times. Local minibuses crawled along cliff-hugging roads, where one wrong move could mean a plunge into the Indus River. We often held our breath as we rounded corners, especially with the children beside us.

But we embraced those challenges as part of daily living. And we had something most of our neighbours didn't: the option to leave the country if we needed to. We had access to resources. If someone got seriously ill, we could fly to a hospital in Thailand. That quiet privilege was always in the background. We didn't speak of it much, but we knew it was there.

And while living in Hunza, our daily life required more effort and teamwork.

Debbie homeschooled our daughters in a small rented room we turned into a classroom. There was no electricity. Each day included routine chores like carrying water from the canal below, chopping wood for cooking, and heating water for bathing and washing.

Some winter mornings, the water in our buckets had frozen overnight. The children, still wrapped in blankets, would sit close to Debbie, waiting for me to light the fire and melt the ice. Those were tender moments, raw, real, and part of the rhythm of our life.

Yet for all the hard work, there was joy. We were in it together.

Our daughters adjusted beautifully to life in the village. As children often do, they blended right in. They dressed like the local kids, played the same games, and formed genuine friendships. In fact, it was often because of them that we received invitations to neighbouring homes for salt tea and light snacks. Their natural openness and laughter helped build bridges faster than any adult conversation ever could.

They became, in many ways, the quiet ambassadors of our family. Through them, people got to know us, and often, to trust us.

What we were building wasn't just a mission, it was a life. Simple, shared, and deeply connected to the people around us.

But through it all, we believed we were exactly where we were meant to be.

Chapter 12

Twelve Years in Six Countries

After two years in Pakistan, we packed up again, older, wiser, and quietly transformed. What began as a leap of faith had become a way of life. Our three daughters had grown accustomed to different climates, languages, and foods. We moved often, adjusting to new landscapes with little more than backpacks, faith, and a fierce commitment to serve.

From 1987 to the late 1990s, we would live and work in four other Southeast and Central Asian countries: Thailand, the Philippines, Mongolia and Malaysia. Each presented unique challenges and deep insights, both practical and spiritual.

This was a season of relentless giving, spiritual passion, and cross-cultural learning. But quietly questions began to take root, and they would one day flower into something that would change everything.

Thailand – Water, Fish, and Simplicity

Our next stop was Thailand, where I worked on a fish pond project to support the Khmer refugees in a refugee camp. The work was hands-on, earthy, and rewarding. There was something deeply satisfying in helping local families sustain themselves with their own resources.

We had no desire to impose Western models. We sought to live alongside, listen, and learn as much as we gave.

Thailand's gentle pace, serene landscapes, and deeply spiritual culture left a mark. Even within the Buddhist framework so different from our own, we found echoes of kindness, community, and moral clarity that mirrored our Christian values.

The line between "saved" and "unsaved" began to feel less certain. We met people who did not share our faith but who radiated a peace and integrity that challenged our assumptions.

The Philippines – Hill Tribes and Humility

In the Philippines, we worked with hill tribe communities, helping with development projects and, yes, engaging in evangelism. We preached the Gospel with sincerity and care, believing, as we had been taught, that without Jesus, these beautiful people were "lost."

I remember one particular moment vividly. While praying for a line of ten people, I reached the last person, a woman who seemed to carry a heavy burden. As I prayed for her, I felt something powerful stir within me, like a surge of energy flowing through me into her. In that moment, she collapsed, overwhelmed, as if the weight she had been carrying had finally lifted.

It was a humbling experience.

Mongolia – The Shifting Ground

Mongolia became one of the most important chapters in our journey.

Debbie taught English, and I worked on a solar cooker project to help reduce dependence on coal and firewood. Later, I focused on planting a local church.

But by then, something inside me had already changed.

I no longer wanted to plant a Western-style church. I felt drawn instead to a simpler, more connected form of gathering, what's often called a **House Church**. In this model, people met in homes during the week, shared meals, sang together, listened to each other, and supported one another like a true spiritual family. Once a week, they might all meet in a larger room, but the focus was always on participation, not performance.

It felt more real. More human. More like the early church in the book of Acts.

And yet, while building something I believed in, I continued to preach that those who didn't accept Jesus Christ were lost. That salvation required a specific belief, a clear decision, a single path.

But deep down, a gnawing uneasiness was starting to grow in my soul, as I started to question many of the Old Testament stories. They depicted a God that wasn't all together so loving as he was part of some, what seemed like, genocidal events. As a result, I mainly spoke from the New Testament Bible.

The more I traveled, the more I met people of other beliefs whose goodness, wisdom, and humility surpassed many

Christian believers I had known. For the first time I was quietly asking myself, "Are they really separated from God?"

I didn't know how to talk about this, not even with fellow missionaries, although there was another missionary who carefully voiced the same question.

For me, it wasn't until our final year in Mongolia that more questions began to take shape. They weren't just passing thoughts anymore. They had become secret doubts, quietly pressing against the edges of my faith.

At the same time, I couldn't ignore what I was seeing in daily life. Many Western missionaries lived quite comfortably, even luxuriously, while working among communities that struggled with poverty. This didn't sit well with me. It seemed out of step with the message we were supposed to be living, one of humility, service, and love. It became harder to believe that religion alone could solve the real issues of inequality and injustice.

What bothered me even more was the constant focus on converting people, along with the rivalry between different Christian groups. Each denomination claimed to have the "true" version of Christianity. Instead of working together, they often competed. This not only confused local people, but it made me question our motives.
Were we really there to serve and love, or just to expand our own beliefs?

These experiences had a deep impact on me. I started to pull back, not from spirituality, but from the organized structures and assumptions of religion. I realised that when something doesn't feel right, we must give ourselves permission to question it. That's how growth begins.

I still believed in God. I still believed in Jesus and in salvation through him. But other beliefs about the Bible being God's Word and the accuracy of Bible stories began not to make sense.

Malaysia and Beyond – The Message Begins to Fracture

While living in Malaysia, I began traveling further afield, places like Siberia and central Indonesia, teaching others about the House Church model. It was something I had started in Mongolia and had become deeply passionate about. I believed this simple way of gathering, where everyone could take part, listen, share, eat together, and support one another, was closer to how the early Christians had lived. It felt more real and meaningful than the formal church services I had grown up with.

But as I continued to visit different places and talk with people, I began to see more clearly how traditional church structures, whether big or small, often didn't encourage genuine community. Leadership was usually centralized. A few people spoke while the rest sat quietly. Most of the congregation didn't participate much. The energy of shared life was missing. More and more, I found myself growing restless, even bored, with the way church was being done, especially the Western-style approach.

I also came to see that not everyone has the same opportunity or freedom to step back and reflect like this. Many people remain caught within the systems and expectations they grew up in, pressured by their peers, communities, or churches to stay the same. But I was slowly stepping outside of those systems. I was beginning to think more independently and to explore ideas beyond what I had been taught.

What I didn't realise then was that a growing number of pastors back in Canada were also quietly wrestling with the same questions. But they couldn't speak up. For many, the church was their only source of income. Doubt had a cost, not just spiritual, but practical and personal.

By this time, I was still occasionally preaching, teaching, and trying to serve faithfully. But inside, the questions were growing louder. My inner struggle with my Christian beliefs and with what I had seen in the missionary world was becoming impossible to ignore.
I was no longer certain that I truly understood the faith I was still trying to live out.

Our Move to Australia

In 1998, after two years in Penang, Malaysia, where our daughters attended a private Christian school, our eldest graduated from high school with honors. She explored university options in Canada and Australia, eventually choosing to study health promotion at a university in Perth, Western Australia. That decision, along with our desire to be close to S.E. Asia, became the turning point for our family. After a short visit to Canada to prepare for the transition, we moved to Perth later that year.

It marked the end of our overseas missionary work, and with it, the support and structure we had known for over a decade. Adjusting to life in Australia, its modern supermarkets, sprawling suburbs, and busy shopping malls, was a culture shift in itself. We settled into the routines of Australian life, but inwardly, my Christian beliefs were no longer as secure as it once had been.

I took a short-term position with a sponsoring church in Perth, but after a year, I needed to find other work. My resume, rooted in overseas development and faith-based projects, didn't easily align with the Australian job market. So I completed a diploma in teaching English, which led to a job teaching migrants. Later, I bought a small business installing TV antennas and telephones. Debb also found work teaching English at a local technical college. It was a new season of rebuilding and adapting.

During this time, we joined a local church community. Outwardly, I slipped back into familiar rhythms of worship and service. But inwardly, I was no longer the man who had left Canada twelve years earlier for Pakistan. The world I had seen, and the goodness I had encountered outside the walls of Christianity, had cracked open the neat framework of my faith. I still prayed. I still believed in love, justice, and grace. But the certainty I once carried was gone.

The church we had joined felt rigid and hierarchical, echoing what I had grown disillusioned with overseas. I shared ideas drawn from our time in Southeast Asia, ideas about small gatherings, shared meals, mutual support, and active participation, but there was little interest in change. So we left.

We found a small house church that better reflected our values. At first, it was refreshing. But after about six months, I began to question some of the theological views being taught. At the same time, my personal doubts were growing. I had seen too much, lived too much, to keep believing things that no longer rang true.

It wasn't easy to process those doubts openly. Most of our friends and family were still committed Christians. I didn't want to offend anyone or cause confusion. So, I stayed involved on the outside, but on the inside, it felt like I was pretending.

Eventually, we stepped away from the house church as well. It wasn't a dramatic break, just a quiet departure, a slow drifting away prompted by the deep sense that something had to change. I didn't know yet what that change would look like. Only that I couldn't keep going as before.

From 2000 to 2004, we moved back to Canada and settled in Calgary, Alberta. Debb taught English, and I started a water filtration business. We wanted to decide once and for all whether we would stay in Canada or make Australia our permanent home. By the fourth winter, as Debb came home from work in minus 35 degree C weather, the decision became clear, we would return to Australia for good.

Amid all these transitions, our family life was flourishing. Each of our three daughters married Australian men, and soon we welcomed grandchildren. In the midst of my quiet spiritual unraveling, there was joy and stability at home. That grounded us.

A few years later, in 2010, we took a one-year contract to teach English in Vietnam. It reignited our desire to return to Southeast Asia and work alongside local communities, but not as missionaries. After completing our time in Vietnam, we returned to Australia and began preparing for a longer-term placement in the region.

Chapter 13

Life After That Morning

In 2012, after years of development work across Asia, and ten years in Australia, plus four years in Canada, Debb and I accepted a new assignment with Australian Volunteers International. We were placed in Yangon, Myanmar, on a two-year contract.
The work was revitalizing as we were once again helping communities in need. Debb trained educators at Yangon University, and I worked with two aid organizations, supporting rural development projects focused on micro-finance and food security. On the surface, I was continuing with the same kind of service I had always offered, helping, supporting, contributing to local wellbeing.

But beneath the surface, something deeper was stirring. Questions I had carried quietly for years were coming closer to the surface, and the safe, familiar framework of my faith was beginning to feel too small for what I was experiencing.

Then in 2012, that morning in Yangon, when I stood at a Men's Breakfast and finally spoke my doubts out loud (the full story in Chapter 7), marked more than just a turning point in my faith, it became the thread that kept pulling me forward. In the weeks and months that followed, I found myself returning to that moment again and again. It wasn't only about leaving something behind; it was the first step into something uncharted, a freer, more open way of living that I didn't yet have words for.

A New Beginning

Myanmar marked the end of one spiritual era, and the beginning of another.

I had spoken the words. I had finally exposed my hidden secret, and it was so freeing.
And I was no longer afraid.

The path ahead was uncertain. But I looked forward to it.

Chapter 14

Freedom in Laos

After Myanmar, we weren't quite ready to return to Australia. The path had shifted, but the journey wasn't over. And so, we accepted one more placement: a two-year contract in southern Laos, a quiet, lush corner of Southeast Asia.

Debb trained English teachers at a local college, and I was assigned to work with the Department of Agriculture, supporting and developing a community cocao planting project with a number of villages. It was simple, steady work, and I absolutely loved it.

And for the first time in years, I felt spiritually at peace. The people I worked with were either Buddhist or free thinkers, and I accepted them as they were. There was no lingering thought of having to convert them. I wasn't working for a church or pushing a particular belief system. I was simply present, living kindly, offering my skills where they were needed, and showing up with open hands and a listening heart. It was great.

Meditation, Silence, and Presence

It was during our time in Laos that I began to explore meditation more deeply. Each morning, before the world awoke, I would sit quietly and listen for the gentle presence of Spirit, that deep sense of connection that seemed to flow through everything.

In that stillness, I would gently let go of the noise in my mind:
The work projects ahead.
The challenges of the day before.
The general living needs for the day.

I would empty myself of all that. It felt like flushing out the clutter of life, creating a clean, open space inside, a return to a neutral wholeness, a place of peace.

And it wasn't about chasing a mystical experience or asking for signs or messages. I wasn't straining to hear words or waiting for a vision.
It was like giving my mind a gentle massage,
A clearing out.
A refreshing.
A sense of feeling lighter, clearer, and ready to move through the day with a calmer heart.

And from that place of peaceful emptiness, I would sometimes receive what I call small gifts,
A quiet insight.
A sense of clarity for the day or the week ahead.
A helpful idea or reminder.

Today I still practice meditation but not as often. During the cold winter months, it's harder to get out of bed to sit and meditate than it is during the warmer summer months. But I am still mindful of the Spiritual presence and connect from time to time.

Looking back, I can see how these quiet moments of meditation prepared me for what would later become the *Kairos* path. It wasn't a sudden revelation, but a slow, unfolding awareness.

The Sacred Presence

I continued to connect with Spirit, not as a being outside myself, but as the presence that infused everything, I call Precious Spirit.

At times during the day, I felt the need to intercede on behalf of a person or situation, not as a theological duty, but as an act of love. I would stop momentarily and quietly lift people in my heart calling on Spirit to provide for the needs of people:

A grieving parent.
A struggling leader.
A child I saw on the street.
Other times, I would call on the Precious Spirit to pour spiritual light into a dark place, a war zone I read about, or a region torn by suffering.

There was no formula, no right words, just the offering of energy, compassion, and spiritual attention.

Laos didn't just mark the end of our overseas work. It marked the integration of everything I had lived and learned. The missionary became the mystic.

Chapter 15

Returning Home, Living the Kairos Way

After two years in Laos, we returned to Australia, not to pick up where we had left off, but to begin a new kind of life.

I carried with me something new: a quiet peace and a clearer sense of who I was. I didn't have all the answers, but I was no longer pretending. I was learning to live with openness, and that, I would later realize, was the beginning of the Kairos path.

We resettled in the countryside, near nature, away from the rush. It was a deliberate choice.

No longer missionaries.
No longer religious leaders.
Just people who had lived, served, wrestled, and arrived at something deeper than belief: a way of being.

A Life Rooted in Simplicity and Spirit

Debb returned to teaching English to migrants, her steady compassion touching lives in quiet ways. I turned toward the outdoors, hiking, archery, biking, as well as volunteering and working with my hands.

The transformation that had begun in Myanmar and deepened in Laos continued to take root. I still prayed, but differently. I still sought wisdom, but from Spirit. And I still felt called, but not to convert, lead, or prove. Only to live truthfully and help where I could.

That, I now believe, is the essence of the Kairos Way.

People Began to Ask

As time passed, conversations began to emerge. Friends, neighbors, former church members, even strangers asked me:

"What are you writing?"
"What do you believe now?"
"Are you still a Christian?"

These questions never bothered me. In fact, they often opened doors to something sacred.

I would answer as honestly and simply as I could:

"I'm sort of a Spiritualist now. I engage with what I call the Precious Spirit, the sacred presence that lives in everything. I still believe in Jesus, but the revolutionary human Jesus and I no longer follow a religion. I follow the path of love, truth, justice, and compassion."

Some nod in quiet agreement. Others are curious. A few were unsettled. But almost everyone listened.

I think some marginally religious people were relieved to hear they weren't alone in their doubts or their longings.

For those curious about how my spiritual beliefs have evolved more deeply over time, I've shared a personal reflection in

Appendix 2 – My Evolving Beliefs and Thoughts and *Appendix 3 – Rethinking Divine Justice.* They offer a simple look at the shifts that helped shape the Kairos path in my life.

The Kairos Path in Daily Life

The Kairos path isn't something that needs a pulpit, a platform, or official approval. It doesn't require robes or rituals, or for someone else to say you're qualified. It's not about belonging to a certain religion or following a set formula.

It's something you live, quietly and intentionally, in the ordinary moments of life.

It looks like this:

- Sitting with someone who is grieving, not trying to fix them, but simply listening with a full heart.
- Speaking truth gently, even when it's not what others want to hear.
- Slowing down to be fully present, offering your time, your hands, or your kindness to someone who needs it.
- Whispering a prayer or calling upon Spirit, not for certainty or control, but for guidance, for help, for light.

I began to see that any moment can be sacred if we approach it with love and attention.

Whether I was planting a tree, writing something meaningful, helping someone in need, or just standing under the night sky in stillness, I could sense the Precious Spirit near.

And slowly, I found myself interceding again, not with big, formal prayers, but with quiet whispers of care:

- "Spirit, be near that father..."
- "Spirit, help this leader make the right decision..."
- "Spirit, bring peace where there is pain..."
- "Spirit, awaken those who cause harm, and show them another way."

I didn't say these things to impress anyone. I said them because my heart was open.

And in that openness, I felt like a vessel for compassion, not because I was special, but because I was present.

That, too, is Kairos.

It's not about performance.
It's not about status.
It's about living with intention, listening for Spirit, and letting love guide your steps, one day at a time.

Even now, the Kairos path continues. Not in loud declarations, but in quiet choices. In how we show up for others, in how we respond to pain, in how we let go, begin again, and trust the Spirit that moves beneath all things.

And now, dear reader, the path shifts again, from mine to yours.

Final Words

A Blessing for the Journey

Thank you for walking with me through the winding road of my story, through the questions, the losses, the awakenings, the letting go, and the slow rediscovery of what is truly sacred.

This book has not only been a story. It has been a journey. A journey of truth-seeking, joy, and becoming.

And now, as we close these pages, the next steps are yours. You may be standing in your own Kairos moment, somewhere between the known and the unknown, between the faith you once held and a deeper spiritual sense that's starting to unfold. You may be distressed from the loss of a belief that once gave your life meaning.
Or perhaps you're awakening to a spiritual path that no longer fits neatly into a single name or tradition.

Wherever you are right now, please hear this clearly:
You are not alone.
You are not lost.
You are not betraying God or goodness by asking hard questions.
You may, in fact, be answering Spirit's invitation to go deeper, to grow, to become more whole.

The Kairos path is not about arriving at a set of final answers. It's about becoming more fully yourself, more alive to the presence of Spirit within and around you, more open to love, more grounded in truth, and more compassionate in how you live.

And as you continue on your path, may this be your compass:
- Walk in love, not fear.
- Be kind and respectful.
- Seek truth, not rigid certainty.
- Act justly, even when it costs you something.
- Welcome difference, without losing your voice.
- Seek commonalities not differences.
- Call upon Spirit, not to control life, but to align with it.
- And always remember: presence is power.

We don't have to figure it all out. We just need the courage to keep walking. This is your moment. This is your Kairos. Walk it with grace.

If you're standing in that tender space between what was and what's next..

For some, finishing a book like this stirs as many questions as it answers. You might be feeling hopeful but also tender, relieved but uncertain. You might simply need to talk, or to know that there are others out there who understand what you're going through.

You might find comfort and connection in these two communities:

- **The Clergy Project** – For current or former religious leaders who have lost faith but still want a confidential, understanding space. *(clergyproject.org)*

- **Recovering From Religion** – For anyone wrestling with doubt, leaving faith, or healing from religious wounds. They offer online support groups, a helpline, and connections to secular-affirming counselors. *(recoveringfromreligion.org)*

You don't have to do this alone. There are kind, thoughtful people ready to listen, to share, and to walk alongside you, wherever your path leads.

Blessings to you, wherever your path takes you.

And if you're curious to know more, the appendices hold the deeper details of my story.

Appendix Introduction

If you've come this far in the book and feel ready to explore more deeply, the following four appendices offer a closer look at the personal journey and reflections that helped shape the Kairos path.

Each one is different in tone and focus:

- **Appendix 1 – These Discoveries Emboldened Me to Leave**
  A straightforward look at the historical, theological, and personal discoveries that led me away from Christianity. These were not small doubts but growing realisations that I could no longer ignore.

- **Appendix 2 – My Evolving Beliefs and Thoughts**
  A personal reflection on how my faith transformed. I share the gradual inner shift from fear-based belief to love-based living, and from religious identity to spiritual freedom.

- **Appendix 3 – Rethinking Divine Justice**
  A thoughtful reconsideration of the violent images of God found in the Bible, and how my understanding of justice has moved from retribution to restoration.

- **Appendix 4 – Final Reflections: Values That Endure**
  A recap of the guiding principles and spiritual values that have stayed with me, even as beliefs have changed. These are values I hope will be useful on your own journey, too.

I want to be clear: none of these appendices are meant to convince or convert. They are offered in a spirit of honesty and companionship.

Take what resonates with your heart. Leave what doesn't. This is your journey, and only you can walk it.

Blessings

Appendix 1

These Discoveries Emboldened Me to Leave

My discoveries have come as a result of reading many books, listening to lectures, and even following debates between traditional Evangelical Christian scholars and those from more progressive, critical-thinking backgrounds, including some who were non-Christian. I didn't agree with everything they said, but much of their insight made sense to me and gave me courage to look deeper. A short list of voices that challenged and shaped my thinking includes: Dr. Peter Enns, Marcus Borg, Dr. John Dominic Crossan, John Shelby Spong, David Felten, Dr. Bart Ehrman, Dr. Diana Butler Bass, Karen Armstrong, Rachel Held Evans, Dr. Elaine Pagels, and Dr. Robin Meyers.

In more recent years, I've also drawn insight from a newer wave of writers and thinkers who have stepped beyond traditional Christianity or reimagined it altogether. Voices like Dr. Valerie Tarico, Catherine Dunphy, Pim van Lommel, Dr. Joshua Bowen, Dr. Bart Erhman and many others on YouTube. These have helped broaden the conversation, addressing issues like purity culture, religious trauma, theology, history and the search for meaning beyond rigid belief systems. While I don't agree with every conclusion they've reached, their questions and honesty have challenged me to keep thinking, keep learning, and keep my life path open.

The insights I share here are only a fraction of the discoveries I've made. There are many more, but I've chosen to limit their number in this book to keep its length reasonable. Still, the list of discoveries continues to grow. You may notice that I haven't always followed the formal format of providing detailed citations. While I have included some references, others come from personal study and accumulated knowledge. I've shared them in a conversational style, as if we were talking over a cup of tea or coffee. This approach may resonate with readers who are reevaluating their spiritual beliefs but prefer thoughtful conversation rather than scholarly debate.

Some people might challenge my points using the Bible, which is understandable. I've seen many debates and have always been struck by how convincing apologists can sound, even when defending ideas that don't make common sense. Arguing with them can feel like debating someone who insists that elephants are hiding in trees, camouflaged perfectly, and who defend their claim by saying, "Nothing is impossible for God." It's nearly impossible to convince someone to see things differently if they're not open to other perspectives. They often create mental walls to protect what they already believe. Thankfully, I've managed to bring down many of those walls in my own thinking.

This journey of discovery has been, and continues to be, one of the most rewarding paths in my life. My interest in archaeology began with my father, who was passionate about ancient history. That early influence helped shape my curiosity about the ancient world. As I explore the vast history of our planet and uncover new archaeological evidence, I've come to realize that the biblical version of Earth's history, which I used to believe, is extremely limited. It doesn't come close to capturing the real depth and breadth of human history.

Some ancient discoveries left me completely amazed. For example, the Barabar caves in India are carved into solid granite with precision that we still can't replicate easily. The Kailasa Temple at Ellora was carved from the top down out of a single massive rock, a feat that would be difficult even with today's technology. These are just a few examples of how incredibly advanced some ancient civilizations were. It makes me wonder where they got their knowledge. Some suggest that other non-human entities may have co-existed with early humans and shared their knowledge. While that idea may sound far-fetched, it's worth keeping an open mind.

Each year, archaeologists uncover new evidence that expands our understanding of ancient history. As more discoveries are made and more questions are asked, we slowly piece together a clearer picture of our past. With the support of professional historians, archaeologists, open-minded theologians, and scholars, my confidence in these findings has grown.

At the same time, I've become skeptical of claims that don't have credible evidence. For example, I no longer believe in stories like Jesus walking on water or Moses parting the Red Sea. These now seem more like symbolic tales or myths created to inspire or serve specific religious purposes. A more likely version, in my view, is that Jesus was walking along the lakeshore, close to the water, and the story grew from there.

In Bible College and church, I was taught to have faith in things we couldn't see. Hebrews 11:1 says, "Now faith is the assurance of things hoped for, the conviction of things not seen." But I've reached a point where I can no longer accept beliefs that go against reason or observable reality. The only exception might be spiritual experiences, positive affirmations, and energy-based practices like Quantum Healing, which I've personally found meaningful and effective.

Here are some of the key questions I often asked myself before I left Christianity:

- If God is loving and in control, why is there so much suffering in the world, even among Christians?
- Why do some Christians, after praying for God's guidance, still end up facing terrible life experiences? Was that God's will?
- Why do Christians praise God for a blessing while other Christians in similar situations suffer or lose everything?
- If God "inhabits the praises of His people," how could 68 people be killed by a bomb in a church while they were singing hymns?
- If the flood covered all the mountains in the biblical story, wouldn't that water have to be fresh? And if so, how did saltwater fish survive?
- How did animals like penguins from Antarctica or kangaroos and koalas from Australia make their way to Noah's Ark in the Middle East?

These questions started to chip away at my trust in the biblical narrative.

I also began to look at archaeological discoveries that directly challenged the Bible's timeline or stories. Here are some examples:

- There is little to no archaeological evidence for a large-scale Hebrew presence or Exodus from Egypt during the time frame the Bible suggests.

- Civilizations like the Sumerians and Babylonians had writings, laws, and spiritual traditions that existed long before the Bible was written. For instance, the Code of Hammurabi, a legal code written around 1754 BCE, predates the laws of Moses by centuries.

- The Babylonian story of Atrahasis includes elements similar to the Genesis story of creation, suggesting that the biblical version may have been adapted from older myths.

- Ancient pyramid structures in places like Mexico and China show that highly advanced cultures existed outside the biblical world, but they're never mentioned in the Bible.

- Göbekli Tepe, a massive ancient temple site in Türkiye, dates back over 12,000 years, well before the Bible's account of human history.

- Fossils of modern humans go back at least 200,000 years, far older than the traditional Christian timeline that places Adam and Eve at around 8,000–10,000 years ago.

- Dinosaur fossils and remains of other prehistoric creatures are found all over the world, yet there's no mention of them in the Bible, even in the story of Noah's Ark, which supposedly included every living creature.

These kinds of discoveries shook my confidence in the Bible as a reliable account of Earth's history.

It's no surprise that archaeological evidence played a major role in leading me to doubt and question my earlier beliefs. As I mentioned earlier, my interest in ancient civilizations came from my father, who was also deeply curious about archaeology. In many ways, it feels like I was born to explore these ancient mysteries and uncover hidden truths.

Let me now share a number of biblical oddities and discoveries from ancient history that made me stop and rethink what I had once accepted without question.

Strange Verses and Inconsistencies in the Old Testament

If you're curious, I suggest reading this article:
"Is the Bible supported by modern archaeology?" by David H. Bailey,
https://www.sciencemeetsreligion.org/theology/bible-archaeology.php
It offers an easy-to-follow breakdown of many archaeological findings that challenge the Bible's historical accuracy.

Here are just a few examples that raised questions for me:

- **Genesis 2:10-12** talks about a river flowing through the land of Havilah where there's good gold and onyx, this is before humans are even created. Why is God concerned about gold and precious stones? What is their purpose at that point?

- **Genesis 2:15-17** tells us that God warned Adam not to eat from the tree of the knowledge of good and evil, saying he would die if he did. But why is the ability to know right from wrong a bad thing? Shouldn't that be a good trait?

- **Genesis 2:21-22** explains how woman was made from Adam's rib after all the animals were created and named. If God is all-knowing, why create all the animals first, only to realize Adam needed a human companion?

- **Genesis 3:1** introduces a talking snake out of nowhere. There's no explanation. It just appears. This sounds more like a fable or myth than a historical event.

- In **Genesis 4**, after Cain kills his brother Abel, he's afraid that "others" will harm him. But where did these other people come from if Adam, Eve, Cain, and Abel were supposedly the only humans alive?

- In **Genesis 6:19**, God tells Noah to take two of every animal onto the ark. But in **Genesis 7:2**, the instructions change, seven pairs of clean animals, and only one pair of unclean ones. That's a big difference. Many scholars believe this is the result of two separate stories being woven together.

- **Genesis 7:19-20** says the floodwaters covered all the mountains of the world, even rising 6.8 meters above the tallest ones. That would include Mt. Everest. I find that very hard to believe. Still, I do think there was a large regional flood, but not a global one.

I remember one day walking with my grandson along the beach, and he asked about Noah's flood. I gently challenged him to think deeper:
"If all the mountains were covered with water, where did that water go after the flood?"

Flood Stories Around the World

Interestingly, many cultures around the globe have their own flood stories. Ancient Mesopotamia, the Chinese, Buddhists, Hindus, Greeks, Aztecs, Aboriginal Australians, and others have recorded flood tales, usually involving a divine warning and the saving of a few chosen people and animals.

The oldest known flood story is the **Epic of Gilgamesh**, dating to around 2700 BCE. In this tale, a man is told by the gods to build a massive round boat, fill it with animals and food, and survive the coming flood. He releases birds to find dry land, just like Noah. So, the question becomes: which version came first? Many Christians insist the Bible's version is original, but historically, it may be the other way around.

Modern geology also supports the idea that around 8,500 to 12,000 years ago, massive floods occurred as ice dams broke at the end of the last Ice Age. Huge land areas were covered with water. These real events may have inspired the ancient stories that eventually became sacred myths.

The Story of Jonah and the Whale

Take Jonah, for example. He's swallowed by a great fish and lives inside it for three days before being spit out alive. This sounds more like symbolic storytelling than actual history. The Bible often blends myth, metaphor, and morality, and understanding this makes it easier to approach these stories with curiosity rather than rigid belief.

Troubling Commands and Violence in the Old Testament

While some biblical stories teach compassion or justice, others deeply troubled me, especially those involving violence ordered by God. Over time, I couldn't reconcile these portrayals with the God of love I believed in.

One of the most disturbing examples is when God commands King Saul to destroy the Amalekites, every man, woman, child, infant, and even animals (1 Samuel 15:3). How could a loving God ask for such complete destruction? Was this truly divine instruction, or was it the voice of an ancient people claiming God was on their side during war?

In Numbers 31, Moses orders the killing of all the Midianite men and non-virgin women, sparing only the virgin girls. And in Joshua, entire cities like Jericho, Ai, and Hazor are said to have been wiped out, men, women, children, all in the name of divine conquest.

Reading these stories, I began to ask myself: *Is this the same God that Jesus spoke of? The one who teaches love, forgiveness, and compassion?* Or were the writers of these books reflecting the cultural norms of ancient tribal warfare and attributing their violence to God?

I found myself thinking, *If one of those Old Testament warriors walked into a church today after slaughtering thousands of people, would he be welcomed?* The idea seems absurd. Yet many believers treat these ancient warriors as heroes of faith.

I came to believe that some of these violent stories may reflect a different kind of spiritual thinking altogether, one rooted in conquest, patriarchy, and control, not in love and wisdom.

New Testament Discoveries and Challenges

Despite all this, I still held onto the New Testament, especially the teachings of Jesus, for some time. But eventually, I began to question even those parts. Not because I rejected Jesus, but because I began to see inconsistencies and later additions to the narrative that complicated what I had once believed to be crystal clear.

Let's begin with some evidence that Jesus existed outside of the Bible:

- **Tacitus**, a respected Roman historian, wrote about Jesus being executed under **Pontius Pilate** and how his followers, called Christians, were blamed for the great fire in Rome during Emperor Nero's time. Tacitus wasn't a Christian and had no reason to invent this.

- **Josephus**, a Jewish historian born just a few years after Jesus' death, also mentioned Jesus. While parts of his writings may have been altered by Christian scribes later, most scholars agree he did refer to Jesus as a real person.

- **Celsus**, a Greek philosopher who was openly critical of Christianity, also wrote about Jesus and his followers in the late 2nd century CE.

So yes, Jesus was a real historical person. But that didn't mean every part of the biblical story about him was literal or original.

Conflicting Birth Stories

According to Matthew 2:1, Jesus was born during the reign of King Herod, who died in 4 BCE. But Luke 2:1-4 places Jesus' birth during the census of Quirinius, which happened around 6 CE, a full ten years later. This conflict made me question how something so important could be so unclear.

The earliest Christian writings, from Paul and the Gospel of Mark, don't mention the virgin birth at all. In fact, Paul says Jesus was "descended from David according to the flesh" (Romans 1:3), which suggests a natural birth.

Later, the Gospel of Matthew refers to Isaiah 7:14 to support the virgin birth. But the Hebrew word *almah* used in Isaiah doesn't actually mean "virgin"; it means "young woman." This mistranslation came from the Greek Septuagint and was passed down into Christian tradition. If this was an honest mistake, it had huge theological consequences.

And Jesus wasn't the only figure with a miraculous birth:

- **Horus** of Egypt was born to the virgin **Isis**.
- **Mithras, Attis, Dionysus, Krishna**, and others were also said to have been born of virgins or divine unions.
- Even **Augustus Caesar** was believed to have descended from a god.
- In **China, Lao-tzu** was said to have been born from the side of a virgin under a tree.

It's clear that miraculous birth stories were common across many cultures, and often used to give spiritual or political legitimacy to a person's life. Jesus's story, while powerful, was not entirely unique.

The Trinity and Other Theological Developments

The idea of the Trinity, God as three persons (Father, Son, and Holy Spirit), was not taught by Jesus. It didn't become official church doctrine until the Council of Constantinople in 360 CE, finalized in 381 CE. That's over three centuries after Jesus' death.

So when people say the Bible clearly teaches the Trinity, it's worth noting that this concept was debated and shaped long after the early Christian community began. Jesus himself likely never claimed to be equal to God in the way later Christians interpreted him to be.

Not All "Paul's Letters" Were Paul's

Only seven letters in the New Testament are widely accepted by scholars as having been written by Paul himself:

1. Romans
2. 1 and 2 Corinthians
3. Galatians
4. Philippians
5. 1 Thessalonians
6. Philemon

The others, such as 1 and 2 Timothy and Titus, were likely written by later followers trying to use Paul's name to add authority. These later letters often present more conservative or hierarchical teachings, especially regarding women, than Paul's original radical message that "there is neither male nor female... for you are all one in Christ Jesus" (Galatians 3:28).

Atonement and Original Sin

For much of my life, I accepted the idea that Jesus had to die for our sins. But even within Christianity, there are multiple theories of atonement. Some focus on ransom, others on moral influence, participation, substitution, or cosmic victory. So, which one is correct?

I now believe that Jesus died because of the sins of certain people in his own time, not as a cosmic transaction for all of humanity. His death, like those of many prophets and truth-tellers, was a result of standing against corruption and power.

As for **Original Sin**, there's no verse in the Bible that clearly teaches we're all born guilty. That idea was introduced by Augustine of Hippo in the 4th century. Before that, the early church saw humanity more in terms of blessing and potential, not guilt.

The alternative view, which I now embrace, is **Original Blessing**, the idea that we are all born with inherent goodness and sacredness. This is a teaching put forth by Matthew Fox, a former Catholic priest who had to leave the church because of his progressive views.

Revelation and the End Times

The Book of Revelation is one of the most misunderstood and misused books in the Bible. It's highly symbolic and was likely written during a time of deep persecution under the Roman Empire.

Some scholars suggest that Chapter 18, which describes the dramatic fall of "Babylon the Great," may not be about a future event at all. Instead, it could be a coded reference to the destruction of Pompeii in 79 CE by Mount Vesuvius, a catastrophic event that shocked the Roman world. The vivid imagery of fire, smoke, and merchants mourning their lost wealth fits that event quite closely.

But many modern preachers treat Revelation as a detailed roadmap for the end of the world, cherry-picking verses to fit their own timelines and scare tactics. I believe this does a disservice to what Revelation truly is: a poetic and prophetic work meant to comfort persecuted people with the hope that justice and goodness will prevail, *not* a literal screenplay for the apocalypse.

Meeting Jesus After Death

Another discovery that challenged me was the differing accounts of where the risen Jesus appeared to his disciples. In Matthew's Gospel, the women at the tomb are told that Jesus will meet the disciples in Galilee, and the story climaxes with the Great Commission on a mountain there. In contrast, Luke's Gospel keeps all the appearances in Jerusalem on the very same day, with Jesus even instructing the disciples not to leave the city until Pentecost. Mark's earliest manuscripts end with no appearances at all, only a promise that the disciples would see Jesus in Galilee, while later editors added material resembling Luke's version. John's Gospel contains both traditions, appearances in Jerusalem followed by a later scene in Galilee, suggesting an effort to hold the two streams together.

For me, this raised the question: if the Gospels cannot even agree on the basic geography of the first resurrection appearances, then we are likely dealing with different versions shaped by each writer's theological perspective rather than a single harmonized historical account. Matthew emphasizes Galilee as the place of new beginnings and mission, while Luke anchors everything in Jerusalem. The fact that these accounts vary so significantly suggests that the resurrection stories developed differently in early Christian communities, each preserving the version that spoke most powerfully to their faith.

When Was the New Testament Written?

Here's something that surprised me: the first written account in the New Testament is widely believed by scholars to be Paul's first letter to the Thessalonians, written around 49–52 CE decades after the original events. And the first gospel to be written, Mark, was not penned until 65-70 CE. That means the stories we read were first passed around orally, often shaped by memory, tradition, and even local customs. Most people at that time couldn't read or write, and there were no voice recorders or newspapers. Over time, these oral traditions were written down, but they had already been reshaped or embellished by years of retelling.

It's not surprising that we find contradictions among the Gospels, differences in timelines, locations, and wording. Each Gospel reflects the beliefs and context of its author and the community they were writing for.

Competing Christianity's and the Council of Nicaea

After Jesus' death, there wasn't one unified group of followers all believing the same thing. In fact, there were many competing interpretations of who Jesus was and what his message meant.

Some groups believed he was divine. Others saw him as a prophet. Some followed Jewish customs, others didn't. Some thought he never had a physical body, while others insisted he was fully human.

To settle the confusion, the Roman Emperor Constantine convened a major gathering of bishops in 325 CE, the Council of Nicaea. His goal was political stability, not necessarily spiritual truth. There were long and heated arguments. The result was the Nicene Creed, a formal statement declaring that Jesus was "of one substance with the Father."

Those who disagreed were labeled heretics and were exiled or excommunicated.

The Council didn't answer every question, though. Over the next few centuries, more councils would follow, debating which books should be in the Bible, how to define the Trinity, and how to punish heresy.

So, when someone today says "the Bible is clear," I have to ask, *which part?* And *according to which council?* What we now call Christianity is the result of centuries of human decisions, political pressures, and theological battles, not a single, divinely downloaded truth.

One Jesus, Many Religions

Today, there are thousands of Christian denominations, all claiming to follow Jesus, but often disagreeing on key doctrines, baptism, salvation, leadership roles, communion, church authority, even the Bible itself. Some say the Bible is literal. Others see it as symbolic. Some believe only a select few are saved. Others preach universal love.

Add to this the many other religions and spiritual paths, each with its own view of God, truth, and life's meaning, and it becomes clear: no single tradition has a monopoly on spiritual insight.

That doesn't mean we must abandon everything. It simply means we can step back, breathe, and reflect.

An Invitation to Explore

I know this has been a lot to take in. You may agree with some of it, and you may strongly disagree with other parts, and that's okay.

My goal in sharing these discoveries isn't to tear anyone's faith down. It's to offer the freedom I found when I started asking honest questions, when I stepped out from behind the fear of being wrong and into the wider mystery of life and Spirit.

I encourage you to read the works of scholars and authors who have walked similar paths, those who have questioned, doubted, deconstructed, and still found a deeper, more universal spirituality on the other side.

If anything here resonates with you, let it be a spark. If it doesn't, you can set it down and move on.

This journey is yours. Walk it with curiosity. Walk it with integrity.

And above all, walk it with love.

Appendix 2

My Evolving Beliefs and Thoughts

Much of my evolving understanding has been shaped by reading and listening to a wide range of thinkers. Alongside my own reflections, I spent time with books, lectures, debates and more progressive questioning voices. While I didn't embrace every idea they shared, many resonated deeply and helped me reimagine what spirituality could mean. Among the voices that most shaped my thinking: Dr. Peter Enns, Marcus Borg, Dr. John Dominic Crossan, John Shelby Spong, David Felten, Dr. Bart Ehrman, Dr. Diana Butler Bass, Karen Armstrong, Rachel Held Evans, Dr. Elaine Pagels, and Dr. Robin Meyers.

In more recent years, I've also drawn insight from a newer wave of writers and thinkers who have stepped beyond traditional Christianity or reimagined it altogether. Voices like Dr. Valerie Tarico, Catherine Dunphy, Pim van Lommel, Dr. Joshua Bowen, Dr. Bart Erhman and many others on YouTube.

These bring fresh perspectives on topics like purity culture, religious trauma, post-evangelical identity, and finding meaning beyond old boundaries. While I don't share every conclusion they've reached, their willingness to question and their openness have inspired me to keep seeking and keep growing.

Leaving Christianity wasn't the end of my spiritual life, it was the beginning of a much deeper, more open journey. This appendix is a snapshot of how my beliefs have gradually changed over the years, moving from a rigid, exclusive system to something more expansive, compassionate, and inclusive.

Some of these changes happened slowly. Others came like a wave. But they all came from a desire to live honestly and lovingly, in alignment with what I was experiencing and discovering, both inside myself and in the world around me.

1. From Certainty to Mystery

In the past, I believed that I had the "right" answers. That's what I was taught. Christianity framed God, salvation, heaven, and truth in black and white terms. There was a clear in-group and out-group. But as I met people of other faiths and no faith, people who were deeply kind, wise, and loving, I began to question that framework.

Now, I see faith not as a system of answers, but as a relationship with mystery, an essence beyond. I don't need to know everything. I don't need to be certain. I just need to stay open, attentive, and willing to grow.

2. From an Exclusive Salvation to Universal Connection

I used to believe that Jesus was the only way to God. But how could a loving Creator exclude the billions of people who never had the chance to hear about Jesus, or who followed other paths with sincerity and love?

Today, I believe the Divine is not confined to one religion or one name. Love, truth, wisdom, they belong to all people, in every culture. I still honour Jesus as a spiritual teacher and a radical example of compassion, but I also find deep value in the teachings of other wisdom keepers who speak the language of Spirit.

3. From a Distant God to an Indwelling Presence

I used to think of God as "out there", a being on a throne who intervened from time to time. My prayers were requests to a higher power, asking for help or forgiveness.

But over time, I began to sense something different. Spirit wasn't far away. It was already here, already within. I now relate to what I call the Precious Spirit, an intimate, loving presence that flows through all of life. It's not a "being" as much as a sacred presence, a quiet whisper in the heart, a deep knowing, a stillness, a connection to all that is.

4. From Fear-Based Faith to Love-Based Living

In the past, fear played a role in my faith, fear of not believing enough, of being left out of heaven or a blessing, fear of being punished by God if I did something bad. Even when love was preached, fear often sat quietly behind it, like a shadow.

But I've come to believe that true spiritual life shouldn't be fear-based. Love cannot flourish in fear. The Spirit doesn't threaten, it invites. It doesn't shame, it awakens. It doesn't separate, it connects.

Now, I try to live guided by love rather than fear. I ask: *Does this belief open my heart or close it? Does it lead to kindness or judgment? Does it lift others or leave them out?* These have become my spiritual compass.

5. From Scripture Alone to Many Sacred Voices

I used to believe the Bible was the only true Word of God. It was sacred, unquestionable, and complete. But over time, I began to see the Bible more as a collection of human stories, powerful, poetic, sometimes wise, sometimes troubling. It reflects the times and cultures in which it was written.

Now I occasionally read the Bible with different eyes. I value some of its beauty and insight, especially the teachings of Jesus. But I also find wisdom in many other places, in nature, in the writings of mystics, poets, scientists, and even in quiet moments of reflection. I no longer believe in one exclusive sacred text. I believe that Spirit speaks in many voices, across time and cultures. If we listen with open hearts, we can hear it anywhere.

6. From Doctrines to Daily Practice

There was a time when I believed that getting the doctrine right was the most important thing. Salvation, I thought, depended on believing the correct theology.

But now, I care more about how I live than what I believe. Right doctrine means little if it doesn't lead to compassion, justice, and humility. I've come to understand that the sacred is found in how I treat others, in how I care for the Earth, in whether I show up with kindness, forgiveness, and generosity.

Instead of obsessing over beliefs, I now focus on daily spiritual practices that ground me such as; stillness, gratitude, honest reflection, meditation, walking in nature, giving without expectation. These things connect me to Spirit in a way no doctrine ever could.

7. From Conversion to Connection

In my earlier years, I believed my main purpose was to convert others, to bring them into the Christian fold so they could be "saved." I carried this belief sincerely, thinking I was helping people. But over time, I began to see how this mindset could also be disrespectful, even harmful.

It placed me in a position of superiority, as if I had truth and others didn't. It treated people not as fellow travelers but as projects to be won over. That began to feel deeply wrong.

Now, I value connection over conversion. I meet people as equals, each with their own journey, their own wisdom, and their own relationship with the Sacred. I no longer feel the need to convince anyone. Instead, I try to listen deeply, to love freely, and to honour the path each person is walking. If something I share helps someone grow, that's beautiful. But if not, that's okay too. True connection doesn't demand sameness, it invites presence and respect.

8. From Obedience to Conscious Living

There was a time when obedience to God, or rather, to how others interpreted God's will, was central to my spiritual life. I was taught to obey church leaders, follow certain rules, and trust that those in authority knew best.

But I've learned that blind obedience can be dangerous. It can lead to spiritual abuse, control, and the silencing of the inner voice. It can make people suppress their questions, ignore their conscience, and live in fear of making a mistake.

These days, I embrace conscious living. I try to live with awareness, integrity, and intention. I don't follow blindly, I weigh, I test, I listen. I've learned to trust my inner wisdom, that quiet sense of alignment or discomfort that Spirit uses to guide me. I still fall short, of course. But I'm not living to impress a distant deity, I'm learning to walk gently, honestly, and with compassion. That, to me, is a sacred life.

9. From Religious Identity to Spiritual Freedom

For 36 years of my life, being a Christian was central to who I was. It shaped my community, my work, my worldview, even my language. Letting go of that identity wasn't easy. It felt like losing part of myself, part of my story.

But over time, I've come to see that my true spiritual self was never limited to one label. It belongs not to a denomination, but to the Great Mystery of life. If anything, for the sake of an identity, I would call myself a Spiritualist.

Now, I don't feel the need to defend a tradition or carry a banner. I simply seek to live in harmony with the Sacred, in whatever form it appears, in love, in beauty, in conscience, in the interconnectedness of all things.

Spiritual freedom doesn't mean I have no roots. It means I've grown beyond the pot I was once planted in. And like a tree reaching for sunlight, I continue to grow, stretching, listening, becoming.

10. Embracing the Possibility of an Afterlife (NDE's)

In recent years, I've found myself more open to contemplating the mystery of an afterlife, not in the traditional doctrinal sense I once accepted, but in light of the many accounts shared by those who've had near-death experiences. These experiences often speak of a radiant light, a presence of boundless love, and a deep sense of reunion with departed loved ones. While I remain cautious with some NDE stories, I no longer dismiss the ones that sound genuine. They resonate with something in my soul, a recognition of the Precious Spirit's embrace, even beyond this life. Whether literal or symbolic, they stir a hope within me that love does not end, and connection to Spirit goes beyond even death in a conscience way.

Living My Values Through Action

Another shift has been more practical. I've moved beyond reflection and belief into more active participation in the world. For me, spirituality must be lived. I now support and volunteer with groups that work to uplift the disadvantaged and protect the natural world. These actions are not just about doing good, they are a way of honouring the sacred in all life. Service, for me, has become a spiritual practice. Whether it's supporting an international aid NGO, planting trees, supporting food programs, or simply showing up where help is needed, I see these acts as expressions of Kairos in motion, where love, justice, and compassion move from thought into action.

Closing Reflection

This journey of evolving beliefs hasn't always been easy. At times, it's been lonely, confusing, even painful. But it's also been incredibly liberating.

I don't have all the answers. I never will. But I no longer need certainty to live a meaningful, spiritual life. I just need to stay awake, to keep questioning, loving, learning, and showing up with an open heart.

If your journey looks different from mine, that's okay. Your path is sacred too. I offer these reflections not as a road map, but as gentle lanterns, points of light from my own walk through the fog.

Wherever you find yourself today, questioning, rebuilding or wondering, may you be surrounded by kindness, guided by Spirit, and rooted in love.

Appendix 3

Rethinking Divine Justice

There was a time when I felt compelled to defend every story in the Bible, even the ones that troubled me. Stories of divine wrath, holy wars, and judgment that fell like fire from heaven. I told myself there had to be a good reason. That God's justice was higher than mine, even if I didn't understand it. That somehow, what looked like violence or cruelty was part of a bigger plan.

But over time, those explanations began to feel hollow.

How could a loving God command genocide? How could compassion coexist with the slaughter of children or the suffering of entire nations? Why would an all-knowing, all-powerful Creator need to completely destroy a, supposed, evil people in order to purify a land? And were they all evil?

These weren't just emotional reactions. They were moral questions, the kind that wouldn't go away. I began to wonder whether some of these disturbing texts might reflect not the Divine's true nature, but the evolving understanding of ancient people living in harsh and dangerous times.

As biblical scholar **Peter Enns** has suggested in his book *The Bible Tells Me So*, the Bible, especially the Old Testament, was never meant to be a flat, one-dimensional rulebook. It's a layered and evolving conversation between humanity and the Divine, **for that period of time**, full of progress, struggle, contradiction, and reinterpretation. Enns argues that much of the Old Testament was written by people who were trying to make sense of trauma, like conquest, exile, and oppression, and who told their stories through the lens of divine action to affirm their survival and identity. In this view, many of the violent images of God, in the Old Testament, reflect how ancient people perceived their God during that time, place, and context. **Not for today**.

These insights gave me new language for something I had long felt. The image of a wrathful, punitive God from long ago, began to fall away, and in its place, I began to see the Sacred Presence of today, not as a distant judge, but as a healing force. A Spirit that does not demand blood, but invites transformation. One that holds people accountable, yes, but always in the context of mercy, growth, and wholeness.

Justice, as I now understand it, is not payback. It is restoration. It is setting things right, not inflicting pain. True justice doesn't require annihilation, it seeks renewal. And the Sacred Presence I now call the Precious Spirit, does not delight in punishment, but in reconciliation.

This shift didn't come easily. It meant letting go of deeply held assumptions and being honest about the violence written into old sacred texts. I don't believe people back then were so evil that their God had to eliminate entire populations.

The Spirit continues to call us beyond fear, beyond violence, toward something deeper, kinder, and more just.

Appendix 4

Final Reflections: Values That Endure

What follows here is a simple distillation of the values and principles that have emerged throughout this journey.
They aren't rules or requirements, but reminders.
They reflect the heart of what the Kairos path has meant to me.

Take them as seeds.
Let them grow in your own way.

Kairos Values That Endure

- **Love over fear**
  Let love, not anxiety, guilt, or obligation, shape your steps.

- **Truth over certainty**
  Stay open. Ask the hard questions. Trust the mystery.

- **Justice with compassion**
  Speak up for what's right, but always hold others in empathy.

- **Presence over performance**
  You don't need to impress Spirit. You just need to show up.

- **Connection over conversion**
  Honour each person's path. Listen more than you speak.

- **Awareness over blind obedience**
  Let conscience and Spirit guide your choices, not just tradition.

- **Diversity without fear**
  Welcome difference. Celebrate the beauty of many paths.

- **Stillness and simplicity**
  Let silence, reflection, and the natural world refresh your soul.

- **Sacredness in the ordinary**
  The Kairos moment is often here, in the quiet, the now, the small.

Closing Note:

This isn't a checklist. It's a compass.
There's no perfect way to live these values, only the daily invitation to return to them.
So take what speaks to you.
Let it settle.
And as you continue your journey, may the Precious Spirit walk with you, quietly, lovingly, always.

Blessings again,

www.ingramcontent.com/pod-product-compliance
Lightning Source LLC
Chambersburg PA
CBHW060401080526
44583CB00012B/412